A Lust *for* Love

My Soul on Paper

(The Untold Story of My Life)

Azure M. Love

A Lust for Love: My Soul on Paper (The Untold Story of My Life)

Printed in the United States of America

Email: a_lust4_love@outlook.com

Print: Powerfully Written Publishing House

600 Lincoln Ave.

P.O. Box 94708

Pasadena, CA 91103

Disclaimer: Age Restriction and Content Sensitivity

This memoir is intended for readers aged 16 and older. Please note that the content of this book may be triggering and offensive to some individuals. Reader discretion is advised.

1. Age Restriction: This memoir contains material that may not be suitable for individuals under the age of 16. It may include explicit language, mature themes, and graphic descriptions. Therefore, it is recommended that individuals under the age of 16 seek parental guidance or permission before accessing or reading this book.

2. Content Sensitivity: The content of this memoir may cover sensitive subjects and evoke strong emotions. It is important to exercise discretion and self-care when reading, as it may trigger or offend some readers.

3. Author's Perspective: This memoir is based on the author's knowledge and recollection. While every effort has been made to present accurate information, some details may be subjective or based on personal interpretation. In order to protect the identity of persons, the name characters have been changed. Rest assured, the author poured their heart and soul into this memoir. The memoir is written in good faith and with pure intentions.

Please be aware of the age restriction and exercise caution when reading this memoir. Understand that the content may be triggering or offensive, and the author's perspective may differ from others. Remember, this memoir is not for the faint of heart. Take it seriously and remember that the author wrote it in good faith. By accessing or reading this memoir, you acknowledge and accept these considerations.

ISBN: 979-8-9859416-1-6

For my mother.

Acknowledgements

There are many individuals who have contributed to and helped me tell this story in some way, and I am forever grateful for the roles that each of them played. First, I would like to thank my mother, who has given me the permission to speak her truth and bring to light the darkness of her fragmented past, so that others can receive hope and restoration.

To my uncle, who is our family historian and my very own hero: you brought to life beautiful memories, which danced across the screen of my imagination. Each of those memories became words written on these pages. Thank you.

To my grandmother: Thank you for leaving behind a legacy of love. You will forever be my best friend.

To my children, whom I love with every part of the fabric of my being: I pray that you may be able to avoid the potholes and pitfalls that I once fell into and live the lives of your dreams.

To my Taochi, my best friend who died far too young: Tash, you demanded that I live life to the fullest, unapologetically. You gave me the permission I needed to freely be Azure and always encouraged me to soar. You will always be a part of my story. Although you are no longer here on this earth, I will carry you in my fondest memories and love you forever, my dear friend.

To my Sister-friends, Amber Hunt, Tameka Cooke, Odette Clancy and Annette Ealy: Where would I be without you? You ladies have been my biggest cheerleaders throughout the conception and completion of this book, and I love you for it.

To my mentor, sister, and life friend, Mrs. Zara Stinson: there would be no book to place in the hands of millions of readers had P.J. not said, "Zara is going to be your mentor." Z, I love, love, love and appreciate you tremendously. You were patient with me as I bore my soul to you. You held onto me during my times of avoidance and procrastination. You were compassionate and shed tears with me as I journeyed back down memory lane to relive the dark tragic days of the past. You were gracious as you encouraged me to be a finisher while we pushed back and delayed deadlines. I bless the divine day we met, and I praise Abba for you!

To Pastor Jonathan DeCuir: thank you! You gave me the gentle nudge in the right direction that I needed to finally sit down and put pen to paper. You always saw more within me than I could see in myself, even as a misguided teenager. I love you, Pastor Jon. "Thank you" truly is not enough. I hope that as you read this book, you will see how the Lord used your purpose to be the solution in my life.

To my mother-in-law, Mrs. Manuella Milton, you are both my mom and my "Naomi." I never knew what it was like to have the nurture, guidance and wisdom of a mother until you came into my life. "Manuella" is not a name I can call you without getting smacked. You have taught me much and shared invaluable lessons about motherhood with me. Thank you for encouraging me to write. No matter the storms of life, please, *"Don't ask me to leave you and turn back. Wherever you go, I will go; wherever you live, I will live. Your people will be my people, and your God will be my God"* (Ruth 1:16).

To you, the reader (yes, you!): thank you. You now hold my soul on paper in your hand. Countless tears have been shed during the writing of this book. In truth, I ran from its completion, and yet it has also been my therapy. It is my deepest desire that as you read my story, you get to glimpse the presence of God.

Finally, to the little girl living inside of me, little Azure: thank you for letting me share your story with the world. I know that it is not a fanciful one to tell. On the contrary, it is a shameful and guilt-ridden one. Yet, you are willing to risk the embarrassment of your choices in order to allow others to look on your wounds and be healed. I pray that we all heal together and that our broken pieces, combined, will display God's masterful work of art.

Lovelust:

The extremely strong and powerful feeling, yearning, craving, and desire to be with someone, know more about them, and have them in your life. That new and wonderful in-love-like feeling that reaches deep down inside and outside your body that you can't get out of your mind, your body, your heart and your soul.
– Urbandictionary.com

Contents

Introduction

What you are about to read is a written work of collected truths: my grandmother's truth, my mother's truth, and finally, my truth. Yet, this truth is not in the sense of what you may think. Though the characters' names have been changed to protect the identity of persons, the nature of this story is true to its essence. This story has been written in order to preserve the memory, life and legacy of my Grammy, who is known in this story as "Lula." Without Grammy, my history would lack adventure, joy and the unquenchable love that I have come to discover. As you read along the pages of this book, you are given the invitation to view the holes within our souls and the truth that has been revealed to us. The truth is, although the journey of our lives has been quite arduous, we have come to discover that we are all worthy of redemption.

The purpose of revealing our truths and experiences with God in this book is to lead you on a journey to understanding the difference between the lust of the flesh and the purest form of love: the love of a Heavenly Father. It is my prayer that our story will lead you to the realization of God's truth; that only He can satisfy your deepest desires. I truly believe that through this book, Abba will not only help you to know and comprehend His love but to discover the inexhaustible grace, mercy and truth that are only found in Jesus Christ. Further, I pray that it will help you to see that because He loves you, He will never leave or forsake you; He will continue to guide, direct and protect you from dangers seen and unseen. He is Light, and no matter what dark road life may take you down, Light will always overtake the darkness.

It is my hope that you will find healing and a deep solace for your soul through every word in this book. May the reading of this written work bring hope and expectation to the lonely, the broken, the empty, the mother who is considering walking out on her family, the lady who just walked into that affair, the young girl who is considering taking her life, and the man who is considering giving up. There is hope for you. Yes, YOU! No matter what confusion may say, there is a bright, glorious, triumphant day yet awaiting you!

CHAPTER 1

Uncle-Dad

"God in His holy dwelling is a father of the fatherless...."

Psalm 68:5a (CSB)

"Troy, it's time!" Lila said as she shook Troy, gently awakening him from his sleep.

"It's time for what, Lila? I've barely had two hours of sleep!" Troy's voice was filled with agitation as he turned over, just in time to find Lila clutching her mountainous belly in agony.

"It's time to have a baby! Hurry! We have to go!" Troy leaped out of the bed, threw on the nearest pair of jeans, and headed straight to the car, being careful not to rush his pregnant sister along.

Troy had anticipated this moment for months! It had begun the day he heard the despair in his little sister's voice as she hopelessly expressed that she was with child. As he drove gingerly down the road trying not to hit a single speed bump too abruptly, he vividly remembered that day. His mind took him on a journey back to Germany where he lived on the U.S. Air Force base. He could still recall the night he'd heard the phone ringing incessantly down the hall. In the darkness and dead of night, no one had the desire or the energy to walk down what seemed to be an endless hallway in the barracks to answer it.

"Hello," an exasperated soldier who had been awakened from his sleep finally answered.

"Hi. May I speak with Troy, please?" a tender voice spoke in a whisper.

"Who's calling?" asked the now annoyed young man who had answered the phone.

"This is Lila." And then there was silence.

An abrupt knock on the door startled Troy who thought he had been dreaming of voices in the night. "Troy, the phone is for you!" That phone call would be forever etched in his memory.

Lila sobbed as she revealed to Troy that she was pregnant by a man who had vanished like a puff of smoke into thin air and that their parents had vowed to disown her if she kept the baby.

"Mom and Dad want me to have an abortion!" she cried. "I can't do it, Troy. I just can't do what they are asking. I don't understand! Why don't they want me to have this baby?"

Troy sat in silence with tears flooding his eyes. He knew the reason behind the why: his parents thought it more fitting to take the baby's life within Lila's womb than to watch their daughter's reckless addiction to cocaine kill both her and their grandchild. He felt a sick feeling in the pit of his stomach as he wrestled with wanting to tell his baby sister the truth, that her toxic love affair with coke might kill her unborn child before it even took its first breath. However, he decided that he loved Lila too much to crush her already-broken heart.

"Lila," Troy began speaking in a hushed voice, "do you want to have this baby, even if you have to raise it alone?"

"Yes, I do, Troy."

"Are you willing to take the best possible care of yourself? I mean, absolutely no smoking, no drinking and no drugs, Lila."

"Yes. Yes, I am!" Lila's voice was filled with determination.

"Okay. Now, promise not to get upset by my next question." Troy spoke hesitantly. "Are you trying to keep the baby because you want to keep the father around?"

Lila took a deep breath. "Troy, when I told him that I was pregnant, he told me that I had to choose between him and the baby. I feel like such a fool! He told me that he already had enough children. When I asked him how many children he had, he said he already had three! I never even knew that he had *one*! I thought he loved me! He said he wanted to marry me, which is the only reason why I stopped taking my birth control in the first place. Troy, he *lied* to me!" Lila's voice leaped out of the phone and echoed down the hall. Her sobs could be heard in the stillness of the night and Troy could feel them in the pit of his stomach. Troy became infuriated with his baby sister for being so gullible and naive, but his heart ached for the defenseless child she now carried.

"Lila, don't worry about Mom and Dad. They will come around. Until then, you and I will raise this kid together."

"You would do that?" Lila's voice turned from hopeless to hopeful in a matter of seconds.

"Yes, as long as I don't get thrown in jail for murdering the guy who got you pregnant." The sound of Troy's own words concerned him. "My job here on the base pays me enough money to help support you and the baby. Living on base allows all of my meals to be provided, so I can save the money I earn. I'll start sending you cash to help you with your needs, and we will raise this baby together."

Lila did not say a word for what felt like an eternity. She sat on the phone in disbelief. An overwhelming sense of unworthiness resonated within her causing tears to spring up and burn her eyes. She sobbed. Lila had never expected her brother to be willing to raise her fatherless child with her. Everyone else was against this pregnancy, so why wasn't he?

"Get some rest, Lila," Troy said. "I will call you in the morning. I love you." Click.

The hallway didn't seem as dark and grim after the phone call, although one thing was certain: Troy and Lila's lives were changed instantaneously.

The next morning, the sun could not have risen sooner. Troy lay in the bed restless and filled with hope at the thought of giving a newborn the opportunity to bring meaning to his world. In the back of Troy's mind lingered concerns about the darkness of Lila's battle with addiction. He knew that one wrong turn could lead Lila down an unspeakable path, straight to the neighborhood drug dealer. It had happened so many times before. All throughout high school, their parents had been there to pick up Lila's broken pieces. They had now grown weary, and their compassion had waxed cold. They now wanted nothing more to do with Lila's addiction, and they were willing to risk abandoning her for a season than to chance losing her for a lifetime.

Troy knew that their parents were right for wanting to protect the baby from Lila's addiction to cocaine. He second-guessed himself, wondering if he had helped Lila make the right choice. What effect would it have on the baby if her lust for drugs spoke louder than her love for her unborn baby? Troy's anxious thoughts filled him with worry. He took a deep breath and thought out loud, "Who knows? Having this baby just might save her life."

CHAPTER 2

A Promise Fulfilled

As a Lovesick lover, I yearn for more of your salvation and for your virtuous promises.

Psalm 119:123 (TPT)

November 23, 1983

Troy flew in from Germany early in the evening. After flying for more than 15 hours from Germany to Charleston, South Carolina, and from Charleston to the Los Angeles airport, Troy was exhausted! Yet, he forced his eyes open in joyful anticipation of seeing his little sister. He was hopeful about making it in time for the delivery of the baby.

When the plane touched ground and rolled up to the gate, Lila and Troy's eyes met from the airplane window. Troy disembarked and eagerly pushed past the slowpokes ahead of him who moved like a herd of baby tortoises. Finally, he greeted his baby sister with a gentle embrace and innumerable kisses on her freckled, golden soft cheek.

With tears in her eyes, Lila said, "Thank you for coming."

"Lila, I told you this is our baby from here on out," Troy replied.

"Do you know how weird that sounds, Troy?" Lila asked.

"I know exactly how it sounds," Troy spoke with a voice of assertiveness. He bent down to say hello to Lila's well-formed belly that looked rather awkward on his 135-pound sister. She was only 22 but had the appearance of a mature woman. Though she seemed frail, Lila looked radiant. Her vanilla brown skin looked like it had been kissed by the sun, or better yet, a sunset. She wore a blush-pink gown as though it were a special occasion. Lila stood a solid 5'7", but her high heels placed her at a model's height of 5'9" tall. Her mahogany brown hair flowed neatly, full of voluminous curls. She was stunning, not in need of a single piece of jewelry or a speck of makeup, and though her belly was round with child, not one person could overlook her beauty. She was captivating. Troy wondered how pregnancy could bring such beauty out of a woman. In disbelief, he wondered how he could even refer to his little sister as a "woman."

The entire car ride home, Troy narrated how he had bravely told his commanding officer at the Air Force base that his sister needed him. He had convincingly given his greatest theatrical performance ever, and to his delight, Troy was given the leave dates he had requested. Now, there he was, the day before Thanksgiving, looking forward to spending time with his family.

Lila spoke of how she had fearlessly stood up to her parents, who had been adamantly against her having the baby. She'd told them, "Troy and I are having this baby regardless of what you think, and we don't want to hear another word about it!" Ever since, Mom and Dad changed their song and dance to "We Are the World" by Michael Jackson; they had stopped hounding her about having the baby, and they were all about love, peace and unity. Troy laughed at the thought of Mom and Dad being silenced by his little sister and felt exceedingly relieved. He took a deep breath and inhaled Lila's fragrance. The sun began to set, and the drive down the 405 freeway was smooth and peaceful. There was a tranquility in the air that seemed unfamiliar to Troy after living on the Air Force base for more than a year.

As soon as they entered the house, Troy's mom, Marie, leaped into his arms, her curly salt-and-pepper hair slapping him in the face. "Oh, how I have missed you!" she shouted, her loud voice resounding in his ear and hurting his eardrum. She squeezed him tightly.

"Mom, you're choking me, and I'm sure that I now have hearing loss in my left ear!" he exclaimed.

Ignoring his comment, Marie let go and held him at arm's length. "Let me take a good look at you! You sure look handsome," she said as she gazed at her son, her voice starting to quiver.

"Mom, please. I just got home. Save the tears for when I have to leave again."

Out of the corner of his eye, Troy saw a tall, dark figure. "Is that my son?" a booming voice rang out, almost startling Troy. The dark figure came out from around the corner. Troy was amazed at how his dad, Raymond, never seemed to age. Looking at the older, dapper gentleman, one would never guess that he had just hit the advanced age of 50. Raymond had a chiseled chin, supple lips and high cheekbones that deemed him the most handsome man on the block. His skin tone resembled a smooth, dark chocolate, a strong contrast from Marie. In fact, Marie was often mistaken for a woman of Caucasian descent. Her fine, curly hair, pale skin, and slender figure often left people staring as she and Ray walked down the street hand in hand, or when they sat down to eat at a restaurant. Their love came with much turmoil, and oftentimes torment.

"Dad!" Troy called out. Troy fell into the arms of his father like a little boy. The two men embraced like long-lost friends.

To Troy's surprise, in walked his big brother from the kitchen. "Robert! I didn't know you were in town," Troy said. "I thought that you were out of town playing baseball for the Oakland A's!"

Robert took after their father – tall, dark, muscular and handsome – while Troy and Lila looked much like their mother with their ivory-toned skin, slender build, and an attractiveness that was lovely to behold. Troy's unique sandy-brown hair and freckled skin had always set him apart from the other guys. Growing up, his distinctive Chico DeBarge looks and kind demeanor made him every girl's dream.

"Man, it didn't work out after all," Robert replied. "I couldn't leave my wife behind."

Troy gave his brother a stern look. "Wife? What wife?"

"Bro, Dee and I got married! After having two kids, I knew I had to make her my wife." Rob's entire face lit up. Every part of his face smiled, including his eyes, eyebrows, and ears.

"Well, congratulations, man!" Troy was equally excited for his brother. "I couldn't be happier for you!" They shared a congratulatory hug.

"Let the man come in! You all have been standing in the doorway letting flies in long enough," Dad interjected with a warm smile.

The house felt warm, and the aroma of a home-cooked meal brought delight to Troy's soul. His room was just as he had left it, with the exception of Mom straightening up a few things here and there. Lila walked in cradling her magnificent belly.

Taking a seat on the waterbed, she leaned back on the pillows and let out a relaxed sigh. "I'm so happy you are here. I told this baby not to come out until you arrived."

Troy's eyes widened. "You can do that?"

"Apparently so, because I haven't gone into labor yet!" Lila chuckled.

That night quickly turned into morning as they sat and reminisced. They laughed so loudly that Mom came in and told them to keep it down.

"Hush, you two! Dad has to go to work in the morning."

"Mom, it *is* morning." Lila's sarcasm caused them to laugh all the more. Marie shook her head and gave a weary smile before gently closing the door behind her.

"Troy, it feels so good to be around someone who shares in my joy." Lila went from smiling to very somber in seconds. "At first, I felt humiliated. I can't believe that I am pregnant by a man who is married."

"Lila, you didn't tell me he was married!" Troy had to remind himself to keep his voice down.

"That's because I was too ashamed of myself for being so ignorant and stupid."

"That is pretty pathetic, Lila," Troy said. He knew it wasn't the best thing to say to his sister in her current state, but he felt the need to express his sentiment. Lila picked up the nearest pillow and threw it at Troy's face, just missing him. "I'm sorry, Lila," he apologized. "Please, continue."

Lila paused, questioning whether she should keep going before continuing. "I should have asked more questions. I should have known that something was off when he wouldn't take my calls after a certain time, and when he did pick up, he would only be able to talk for a few minutes. I was too infatuated with him to pay attention to the signs." Lila covered her face with her hands as if she wanted to make herself disappear. She slowly let out a long sigh and said, "Troy, he made me feel like a phenomenal woman."

"Lila, don't you know that that is exactly what you are? A phenomenon is all I see when I look at you," Troy said, reassuring his baby sister.

"Thank you, Troy. But I've never had a man treat me like he would lasso the moon *and* the stars just for me." There was a deep, penetrating silence before she continued. "That's how he made me feel, and that is who he made me believe I was to him. Truth be told, I hate that I miss him! I hate that I miss the scent of his cologne or looking at him walk towards me after I have been waiting anxiously for him to arrive."

Troy could hear the deep longing in her voice as she spoke. Although Lila appeared to be present, he could tell that she had found solace in the memory of a distant lover. "I have to say that this pregnancy has been a beautiful distraction," Lila said as her thoughts came back into perspective. "All I can think about is seeing my baby smile for the first time, and it all seems worth it."

Troy sat in silence as he watched his sister intently. In the dim light, he could see that his sister still fought a war against the enemy of addiction. Marijuana had been Lila's drug of choice for a long while before being introduced to cocaine by her best friend. In high school, the two would often get caught by the janitor smoking weed in the girl's bathroom. That's where it all started. The sting Troy felt in the pit of his stomach at the thought of these memories was soothed as he watched his little sister rub her belly with the caress of a mother's love. She looked at her stomach smiling, as though she could see right into her womb to the baby.

Lila looked up and passionately said, "Troy, you are a hero. You saved this baby's life, and I think this baby is also saving mine."

CHAPTER 3

The Birthing

When a woman is about to give birth, she is in great pain.
But after it is all over, she forgets the pain and is happy,
because she has brought a child into the world.

John 16:21 (CEV)

November 24, 1983

"Are we almost there?" Lila moaned and groaned with every stop and turn. Troy could barely keep his eyes open after only getting two hours of sleep. While traveling the 14 hours from Germany to California, Troy had stayed awake the entire time in anticipation of this moment. Now, he struggled to keep his eyes on the road. He was beginning to regret staying up all night, talking, laughing and shedding tears with Lila. Troy tried his best to remember the way to the hospital. *"Maybe I could focus better if I had gotten some sleep,"* he murmured within himself. *"If only this baby had decided to come a few hours later... better yet, a few days later."*

Just then, Troy looked over at Lila, who was moaning in agony, and he managed to smile. He realized that he had made it in time for the delivery, after all. It was Thanksgiving Day and Troy made a mental note of the date: November 24, 1983. This would be a historical date that he would cherish forever. *Is this what it feels like to be a father? If so, how could a man cause a woman to choose between him and his child? This has to be one of life's greatest moments.*

Troy's thoughts were interrupted by Lila. "Troy, hurry!" Lila's soft moan had now turned into a wail. Her shriek shocked Troy back into reality. Within moments, they were pulling up to the hospital. "Troy!" was all that Lila could manage to bellow out as they wheeled her into Labor and Delivery.

Troy waited frantically in the waiting room after learning that his sister had to be rushed into surgery. The young female doctor shared the news with Troy that the baby would not come down the birthing canal naturally. Instead, they would have to perform a cesarean section on Lila. Troy had never heard of such a word before that moment.

"Doctor, just make sure they are both taken care of... *please*," Troy pleaded with a voice of concern. The doctor gave a gentle nod before walking away.

Troy paced back and forth down the hall wondering what he should do next. He fought back the urge to cry, uncertain of why. "Am I excited or am I just being emotional?" He silently asked himself. Troy looked up to find his mom and dad clinging to one another as they walked towards him. Marie looked excited while Raymond looked stoic. Troy embraced his dad and began to frantically say,

"The doctor said she has to have some sort of surgery. The baby isn't coming out. I feel so helpless, like I should be doing something, but I don't know what to do!"

Marie let out a soft laugh.

"Marie, don't laugh at the boy. He hasn't had any children yet," Raymond quickly said, coming to his son's defense.

"Oh, I'm only laughing because he reminds me so much of his father," Marie snickered as she gave Raymond the side-eye. She placed her hand on Troy's heart. "They're going to be fine," she said. Her words seemed to still his anxious heartbeat.

The surgical room door flew open. A glowing smile radiated off the face of the very lovely doctor. "Are you ready to meet the princess?" she asked.

"Princess? It's a girl? It's a girl!" Troy repeated himself as though he had not heard himself the first time. Marie laughed once more, but Troy did not look back; he began to bolt straight ahead towards the door to see his sister and her new arrival.

"Hold on now, fella," Dad said, grabbing his arm. "You're moving so fast that you're going to miss this moment." Troy gave him a bewildered look. "Take a deep breath, Troy. Relish this moment. If you move too swiftly, you will have missed the whole thing. Trust me, I know. I was just like you when your brother was born. I couldn't wait to see him for the first time. Now, look at all the years that have passed since then. All I have are the moments, now memories, that I've been gifted to see." Raymond paused as though he wasn't sure if he should share his next thought.

"I know that you have been supporting Lila and encouraging her during this difficult time," he continued. "You make me a proud father. I want you to know that I am ashamed of how your mother and I handled the news. We were ready to give up on Lila, but you saw hope when your mom and I could not. We were looking through eyes of fear, while you saw through eyes of faith. You have always had this overwhelming love that simply radiates within you. Now, this baby is here because you shared that same love with your sister. You saved a life today, Troy, and even if the military never recognizes it, you are a hero."

Troy looked his dad in the eye. "Dad, Lila said the same thing, but in all fairness, I'm no hero. I just knew that I would not be able to live with myself knowing that this innocent child had to die for sins she didn't even commit. It's not her fault. It's not her fault, Dad!" By now, both Troy and Raymond were moved to tears. Every emotion that Troy had been restraining had risen to the surface and broken through, making way for a flood.

"Pull yourself together," Raymond said. "I didn't tell you to go crying on me. We haven't even seen the baby yet!" He grinned while wiping a tear away from his own eye.

"Thanks, Dad." Father and son embraced, took a deep breath and walked toward the room where both Lila and the princess awaited.

CHAPTER 4

Zoe Maree

"The Lord called me from the womb; from the body of my mother, He named me."

Isaiah 49:1b (MEV)

November 26, 1983

Delivering a baby is excruciating, Lila thought to herself as she lay in the hospital bed. She wished that the father of her fatherless child would walk through the door of her room. It had been two whole days since the birth of their daughter, and he had yet to appear. Lila felt foolish for wanting him to be there with her. Just then, there was a gentle knock on the door.

"Come in!" Lila's hushed voice called out from behind the curtain. A mysterious person walked in holding an armful of pink roses and a bouquet of pink balloons, which hid the mystery man's face. The balloons floated in the air such as to announce, *It's a girl!* A plush pink teddy bear held a pillow that read, "Welcome, precious baby girl!" Slowly, the roses lowered, revealing a wide-eyed, bright-smiling Troy, who looked freshly shaven and refreshed as a result of a full night's rest.

"You're full of surprises, aren't you?" Lila managed to smile, although she still felt tired, groggy, and a tad disappointed that it wasn't *him*.

"I figured after watching my little sister almost birth my niece in the car, you deserved the entire gift shop, but the lady at the counter told me that I had to leave some things for the next customer!" With all of the gifts and balloons he carried, Troy looked like three holidays rolled into one.

"Troy," Lila began as she made a failed attempt to sit upright in bed, "thank you for making sure we got here safely. I know you were tired after such a long day, yet you managed to get us here in one piece." Lila's voice made her sound more fragile than she appeared. "When I think about it, I must have been in labor all day. I just didn't realize it, because it was overshadowed by the joy I felt seeing you." Lila gave a weary smile. "The doctor told me that had I waited any longer to get here, the baby would have certainly been born in the car."

Troy raised his eyebrows. With a half-smile, he said, "Not in *my* car!"

Just then, the sound of two men arguing could be heard coming from the hallway. "I'm here to see my wife," said one of the deep voices.

"She's, *my* wife! Tell me where I can find *my* wife!" said a different, more distinctive voice.

Troy looked confused as he hesitantly peeked his head out the door towards the nurse's station where the men stood. He recognized the voices of the two men who seemed to be arguing but playing at the same time. Troy hoped that he was mistaken about whose voices they might be. He stepped into the hallway only to discover both of his best friends causing a huge scene. Frank and Howard pushed and shoved one another as they demanded an answer from the puzzled nurses. Troy shook his head at the sight. He sat the gifts down on a nearby table, and with a voice louder than all said, "Hey, cut it out! She's in here."

The two men followed Troy down the hall, leaving the nurses in a state of confusion.

"Hey, baby!" said Frank as he entered the room. Troy shoved Frank, causing him to trip over his own two feet. The three men laughed.

"Bro, are you trying to get us all kicked out of here?" Troy asked, giving his friends a look of disbelief.

"Man, we were just saying on the way up here that if you weren't our best friend, one of us would have won Lila's heart by now," Howard said, as he puffed out his chest like a male peacock flaunting his feathers.

"Well, both of you would be disappointed, because I don't go for guys who compete for attention." Lila's response left the men stunned.

After a moment of awkward silence, Howard said, "Well, which one of us does the baby look like the most?"

Troy let out a wallowing laugh that could be heard from a few rooms over. "Neither!" Troy interjected. "The baby is light skinned with blue eyes. Neither one of you negroes fits that description!" His two friends joined him in laughter.

"Hey!" Lila said, feeling the need to intervene. "That's my baby that you are talking about!"

"And now, it's our baby Lila," Troy replied. "I just didn't know you had a thing for white boys!" The room filled with unrestrained laughter. Lila briefly joined in but could not bear to laugh due to the pain it caused.

"I hear the sound of celebration happening in here!" Marie said, as she walked into the room.

"Mom, they're talking about my baby," Lila said in her all-too-familiar "I'm telling" voice.

"Well, what are they saying?" Marie questioned with curiosity.

"They said because my baby was born with light skin and blue eyes that she's white!"

"Now, don't be ridiculous, boys. We all know that my daughter takes after her mother. She likes them tall, dark and handsome," Marie said with a glowing smile. "Besides, my grandbaby is absolutely gorgeous!" Marie smiled warmly, like a proud grandma before continuing. "I decided that I am going to have her call me, Lula."

"Lula?" Troy and Lila questioned with the sound of one voice.

"*Yes*, Lula," Marie answered confidently.

"Where did you get Lula from, Mom? Your two older grandchildren don't call you that?" Troy asked questionably.

Marie turned and looked at Troy with watery eyes and said, "I just heard the cutest little girl talking to her grandma in the lobby as I waited on the elevator downstairs. She called her grandma, Lula, and it touched my heart. When I asked what Lula means, the petite grandma answered, 'Famous Warrior'. It was the way she said it that I admired most. I imagined her standing with a sword and shield in her hand, fiercely protecting her little one with honor. That is when I decided, that's what my newest grandbaby will call me – Lula."

"Wow Mom, I never knew you had such a vivid imagination!" Troy said as he began to take the stance of a warrior proceeding into battle. Everyone in the room erupted into laughter once more. Marie shook her head and took a seat in the chair beside Lila's bed. An abrupt knock on the door caused all heads to turn synchronously. Just then, a strikingly beautiful female doctor entered. "Hi, everyone! May I do a quick vital check on my patient, please?"

"Sure," all the men replied with one voice. Marie gave a stern look to Troy, as if to say, *Take the guys, but I am staying right here.* The men got the hint and stepped out of the room.

"So," the doctor began, "which one of those fine brotha's is the real Mr. Love?"

Lila laughed softly. "None of them. The one who brought in the roses is my brother, and the other two are his best friends."

The doctor abruptly paused her exam and looked at Lila. "Does that mean they are all available? The nurses want to know!" The women laughed.

Marie replied, "All but one. Leave the light-skinned one with sandy-blond hair alone. That's my son."

"Yes, ma'am!" The doctor kindly replied, smiling. "Lila, the nurse will come in shortly with your discharge papers. You're going home today!"

"I'm so glad to hear that. I miss my bed," Lila moaned while shifting into a more comfortable position.

"I do need to make you aware that the baby will have to stay here for observation," the doctor added.

"Observation?" Lila sat up straight in her bed, forgetting about the pain in her abdomen.

"Yes, Lila." The doctor glanced over at Marie and then back at Lila. "Is it okay for me to speak with you while your mother is present?"

"Of course!" Lila replied.

The doctor took a seat at the foot of Lila's bed. "Though you carried her to full term, your baby was only four pounds and five ounces. We need to keep her here until she is at least five pounds." The doctor looked over at Marie and hesitated before continuing. "There is one other concern, Lila."

Lila anxiously awaited the doctor's next statement. "We found traces of a narcotic in the baby's blood. Is there a chance that you happened to take any drugs while you were pregnant?"

Lila's heart dropped and she began to panic. "What's wrong with my baby? Did I hurt her? Is she okay?"

The doctor spoke in a calming voice. "That's why I am asking these questions, Lila. She seems to be having some type of withdrawal. I need to know if you took anything, so I can properly treat her."

Lila did not look up as she confessed to the doctor that she had fought the urge not to use cocaine throughout her entire pregnancy, but there were times that she had slipped and did not win the battle. She admitted that she had smoked marijuana here and there also, but she didn't think that she had done it enough to hurt the baby. Marie stood up and walked towards the hospital window, staring, as though she hadn't heard a single word. Lila glanced over at her mom but knew that she had to tell the truth for the baby's sake.

"Please, doctor, is she going to be okay?" Lila cried.

"We are doing everything in our power to make sure you get to take her home soon, because that's where she belongs – with you," the doctor answered.

Lila could not understand why the doctor would say such a thing after her confession. Lila could barely hold back the tears of shame and defeat. "How long will she have to stay here before I can take her home?" Lila asked. "Please, doctor,

I can't leave her here alone!" The baby was only two days old, and Lila already felt like a horrible mother.

"We are working hard to make sure that she receives the proper treatment for her withdrawal symptoms, and we are closely monitoring her progress. The baby will also need to be able to breathe on her own and drink from the bottle before we can release her. Right now, she has to be fed through a tube which will help her gain a few more pounds and receive the proper nutrients she needs."

Lila's heart broke afresh with every word, knowing that she was responsible for the suffering of her baby girl. She curled up in a ball and wept, ignoring the piercing pain she felt in her abdomen with every sob.

Troy heard weeping and ran inside. "What's going on?" he asked with marked concern. Marie gave Troy a *"not right now"* look.

"Don't worry Lila," the doctor assured. "Your baby is getting the best possible care. All of the nurses love her already. They say that she is the most beautiful baby they have ever seen with her sky-blue eyes." The doctor placed a gentle hand on Lila's shoulder before she began to leave the room. Stopping at the door, the doctor turned and asked, "What did you decide to name her?"

Lila brushed her tears away before replying. "Zoe. It means 'life'. I gave her the middle name, Maree, after my mother." Marie could no longer stand in silence. She buried her face in her hands and wept, still facing the window, feeling a deep sorrow mixed with joy at the thought that her granddaughter would carry her name. Now, she understood why she felt the need to protect Zoe and become her 'famous warrior'. Troy walked over to his mother, whom he rarely saw cry, and placed his hand on her shoulder. Lila watched and then continued.

"Her name is Zoe Maree Love."

"Love?" The doctor seemed pleasantly surprised. "I see you gave her your last name. It's beautiful and so fitting." The doctor smiled radiantly while gently closing the door behind her.

CHAPTER 5

My Lula

Love never brings fear, for fear is always related to punishment. But love's perfection drives the fear of punishment far from our hearts.
1 John 4:18 (TPT)

Present Day: Lula, Mama, and Me

I, Zoe Maree, discovered my first love in the person of Marie Grace Love, my lovely grandmother, whom I affectionately referred to as "Lula." My Lula often reminded me of the most beautiful hummingbird: bright, radiant, and adventurous. It's hard to tell where hummingbirds are going or where they have been. Their flight pattern bounces up and down, back and forth; here and there as though they have been everywhere. They are aptly named "hummingbirds," and for good reason: the humming sound that they make as they whiz past you is unmistakable. It is a subtle sound that could easily go unheard by most, but it is all-too-familiar and easily perceptible to me.

Lula and I could always hear the hummingbirds coming. We would stop and stare at the magnificent, colorful creatures and try to guess which flower's nectar the hummingbirds would drink of next. They are glorious, mesmerizing, and delightful to observe. That was my Lula. She had a striking beauty that made people want to stare at her for long periods of time. Her wavy salt-and-pepper hair and bright skinned complexion made her look very distinguished. She was always smiling and always graceful. Like hummingbirds, Lula was mysterious and curious, and her life was full of adventure. However, unlike hummingbirds, Lula did *not* mate for life.

I called her "Lula," which means "famous warrior." All others knew her as "Marie" which means "bitter." Marie was no name for my Lula, for there was no trace of bitterness in her, at least not in my youthful eyes. Lula's soul exuded love, kindness and a remarkable brilliance. Lula was my best friend, and I was her heartbeat. Together, we danced to a cadence called the rhythm of life, and we didn't care if others were looking. She was always a radiant light to my darkness, and I was the joy of her life.

As a little girl, Marie had the all-too-familiar longings that most young fatherless girls have. Although Marie knew her father, he was a man given to alcohol. He was an African American man whose brown skin was forbidden around her simple, yet beautiful Caucasian mother. The young Marie often wondered if this was the reason why her mother had given Marie and her older sister, Clara, over to be taken care of by Aunt Nettie, her mother's sister, when Marie was around seven years old. The two young sisters lived with Aunt Nettie in a small town called Lake Elsinore and soon began to love life on the ranch. Over time, Marie developed a deep affection for horses and found solace on the lake. Her aunt, Nettie, was tender and attentive to both Marie and her sister, Clara. Marie became a free bird; she learned how to use her wings and was given the permission to soar.

After a few years of living with Aunt Nettie, Nettie's sister, Nora, came to help take care of the two girls. Marie and Clara were born during the era when being light skinned came with its privileges. Marie received many, while her brown-skinned sister, Clara, did not. It was not long before Marie recognized the indifference with which her big sister, Clara was being treated, because of her brown skin. As they grew older, it became harder for her Aunt Nettie to decide which school the girls would attend, since Marie passed for white, while Clara was obviously black. Further, both Aunt Nettie and Aunt Nora were fair skinned and had never really had any trouble with the neighbors until their darker-skinned niece Clara came to town. The townspeople's smiles immediately turned to frowns of disapproval when they saw Clara coming. Their obvious contempt for her, blatantly expressed by the shaking of their heads, the contortion of their faces, and the turning up of their noses as if there was a foul stench in the air, signaled their disdain for the presence of someone of Clara's complexion in their otherwise proudly light-skinned community.

To make matters worse, the townspeople were not the only people who had low regard for Clara; their Aunt Nora was also mean to her for no apparent reason. This mistreatment suffered at the hands of someone who was supposed to protect and love them unconditionally, chiseled away at Clara and Marie's young souls. Although Marie enjoyed the preferential treatment she received, it came at the price of her beloved sister's tears, making her life terribly bittersweet. Aunt Nora treated Clara with disdain yet favored Marie, as if being abandoned by their parents were not enough. As a result, the once bubbly and bright Clara now hardly ever spoke and was given over to isolation and loneliness. Because of this, their time in Lake Elsinore went from the best time of Marie's young life, to the worst.

My Lula's beautiful wings were clipped, and her aunt Nora made sure of it. Marie yearned for the stability of a family who would care for her and her sister like loving parents. She often dreamt of what it would feel like to be loved by her father, adored by her mother, and accepted by society. The once beautiful, bouncing hummingbird was now grounded, and Lula grew up with a spirit that was broken and distorted. That brokenness would be passed down from one generation to another: from Lula to my mama, Lila, and ultimately, to me, Zoe Maree.

CHAPTER 6

The Hummingbird

You are only truly happy when you walk in total integrity, walking in the light of God's Word.

Psalm 119:1 (TPT)

Present Day

I lost track of how many times my Lula moved and changed her address from one place to the next. Like the hummingbird, she floated from place to place, each time creating a new pathway on her endless journey. Lula loved to visit the beaches and would often find her home near the ocean. "Let's go on a bike ride, Zoe." Lula would say, and together we would ride our bikes to the lagoon and the pier, discovering lively restaurants along the way that we would often frequent.

When I was about four years old, Mama took me to Lula's for a visit. Lula lived in Long Beach, California at the time in an immaculate, three-story townhouse. Lula's home always reminded me of a museum filled with our family's history. One day, Lula and I were in her bedroom upstairs. Lula was in the bathroom getting ready for yet another adventure and like any ordinary joyful four-year-old, I started jumping on the bed. Suddenly, there was an earthquake. My first ever to be exact. Lula came running out of the bathroom. I fell on the bed and with a loud voice shouted, "Lula, God's knocking on the front door!" All Lula could do was laugh, house rumbling and all.

My Lula and I went everywhere together gathering beautiful memories. As the years went by and my growth evolved, we began to get lost on purpose and call these escapades "adventures." At the ripe age of 11, most of our adventures involved Lula teaching me how to drive her 1984 silver Hyundai Excel. Lula always said that if I learned how to drive a stick shift first, I would be able to drive anything. During my first lesson, Lula placed my hands on the joystick and let me feel the rhythm of the car shifting into gears. Not long after, I was sitting in the driver's seat, learning how to use the pedals while Lula shifted the car into gear. I would find any and every reason to hop in the car with Lula, just so that I could drive. Back then, it was not unusual for an 11-year-old to be behind the wheel of a vehicle, so, when Lula came to visit, I knew if I begged and pleaded long enough, she would eventually say with bright eyes, "Okay. Let's go!"

It wasn't long before I was driving Lula around town, venturing to liquor stores, and visiting her guy friends who were always very nice to me and never let me leave empty-handed. They would butter me up with handfuls of candies and compliments.

"Well, you have a beautiful granddaughter, Marie," I heard one gentleman say. He looked at her with lustful desire and whispered, "She takes after her grandmother." Lula was the epitome of a sunny day at the beach, and it seemed that the men we came across loved soaking in the rays of her sunshine.

My Lula often said, "The day I met your grandfather was a day of awe and wonder." Everyone called him "Ray," although his mother named him "Raymond Eugene Love." As Lula described him, Ray was marvelously wonderful. He was the most handsome brown-skinned brotha that she had ever laid her eyes on, and not only was he fine, but he loved taking Lula for a spin in his classic cars.

The two high school sweethearts were the talk of the town. They made a handsome couple. Grampa made sure that Lula knew exactly what she meant to him and how much of a treasure she was in his eyes. He did not hesitate to express his affection for his beloved Marie. They fell in love quickly, and their future together was inevitable. It was not long before Raymond Love introduced Marie to his mom, my great grandmother, Great Grammy K. She was a lovable Christian woman whose eyes were bright; somewhere in the middle of copper and hazel, and she always wore a smile.

Walking into the Love family home was just that: a house filled with love. It was the family atmosphere of which Lula had always yearned for and dreamed. Being with Ray made Lula's empty soul feel complete and whole. The two became one shortly after high school, and their love blossomed into a beautiful family. Three babies later with the love of her life by her side, Lula felt she had all her heart could desire, and life could not get much sweeter, or so she thought.

It was not until I grew older that I began to notice the shadows under my Lula's eyes. Before I was born, somewhere along Lula's insatiable quest for belonging and adventure, she had lost something invaluable: herself. She became discontented within her marriage, and although she had birthed some of the world's most beautiful children, she became dissatisfied as a mother. She longed for more. Grampa was old school and very systematic. He did not care for change, and he most certainly was no hummingbird. He was mellow and ran a tight ship. There was a vast contrast between Lula's spontaneous nature and Grampa's need for structure. While he was, by far, the most handsome man she had ever seen, Grampa's militant style and stern discipline made him more and more unattractive to Lula, while Lula's whimsical spontaneity caused her to seem irresponsible and become unappealing to Grampa. Life together became a life of continual arguing, and their love turned into hostility; all the while, their children would grow up not knowing the natural affection expressed between their mother and father. At a price, they could not afford to pay.

Marie didn't know how to express the turmoil she felt within. She began to feel worthless and was often fighting the darkness of depression. She felt invisible, like her thoughts and opinions were not valuable and did not matter or carry weight with her husband. *Cook, clean, entertain three small children, repeat. Don't think, just do. Don't complain, because this is the life you wanted. Right, Marie?* Her own distracting thoughts plagued her mind, and soon after, her beauty faded, her smile disappeared, and Marie was cloaked with invisibility. Hummingbirds are not meant to be caged, and neither was my Lula.

On difficult days, Marie would go for a walk around the block to clear her mind. Just around the bend lived Mr. Richard Clemmons, a charming neighbor. He was kind, gentle, and looked at Marie with the same longing in his eyes for freedom and adventure that she felt within her own soul, which magnetized the two. The nurturer in her wanted to tend to his wounds, caused by years of neglect, as he also soothed hers. Soon, the two fell into a lustful trance but called it love. For once, there was someone who loved to hear the sound of her voice, which made her long for his conversation. They would stand in the yard talking for hours, laughing and carrying on while his wife was at work.

Lula became an invaluable presence in his life. He wanted more, and so did she. There was only one problem: he was a married man, and Lula, a married woman. Their desire for each other caused him to denounce his wife and they secretly swore to love one another for all of eternity. He promised to marry Lula after divorcing his wife. Together, they developed a plan, and both Lula and her lover were going to get married after both of their divorces were final. Unfortunately, his actions never seemed to match his words. As she waited for the fulfillment of his empty promise, Marie's love turned into rage, causing her to fall deeply into a loveless depression.

There's a familiar and true saying that "Hurt people, hurt other people." Although her lover's promise remained in default, Lula broke Grampa's heart when she decided to tell him that her lust for another man spoke louder than her love for him. Lula shattered his world. Grampa possessed a love for her that was genuine and a commitment that was unwavering. I often wonder what it was within my Lula that kept her from being capable of the same.

CHAPTER 7

Untreated Trauma

For love is as strong as death, its jealousy as unrelenting as Sheol. Its sparks are fiery flames, the fiercest blaze of all. Mighty waters cannot quench love; rivers cannot sweep it away. If a man were to give all the wealth of his house for love, his offer would be utterly scorned.

Song of Solomon 8:6, 7 (BSB)

Winter of 1984

"Lila, you have a phone call," the bank manager said to Lila's surprise.

"Thank you, sir!" She nervously smiled as she hurried to the back office, where the person on the other end of the phone call awaited. "This is Lila speaking," she said hurriedly.

"Lila, it's Troy." Lila was taken aback. Troy knew not to call her at work. She had told him this repeatedly ever since she had learned that personal phone calls could jeopardize her new job at the bank. "I know I'm not supposed to call you at work, but it's an emergency. I need you to go home and check on Mom."

Lila's heart sank. "Why?" was all that her nerves allowed her to ask.

"Because I'm in Germany! I would do it myself if it didn't take more than 14 hours to get there."

Lila let out a sigh of annoyance. "Troy," Lila began, "I don't have time for this. I'm not even supposed to be on the phone." Lila spoke in an aggravated whisper as she looked around the office and caught a glimpse of her co-worker giving her a stern look. "Troy, I gotta go. Whatever it is, it will have to wait. I'm sure Mom is fine."

"Lila!" Troy was now shouting from the other end of the phone. "Mr. Clemmons shot and killed his wife just before turning the gun on himself!" Lila's mouth dropped and so did the phone. She didn't even think to hang it up as she rushed to grab her purse and coat while scurrying to the door.

"Ms. Love, is everything alright?" she heard her boss call out from behind her.

"Uh, I don't know? I just got word of a terrible family emergency. May I please be excused for the remainder of the day?" Lila had not been on the job long enough to request time off and was still on her probationary period. Her boss was a no-nonsense kind of guy, but Lila knew that she had to get to her mom before the news of her lover's death did.

After a long pause, her boss quietly said, "Go on, and keep us posted. I hope everything is okay with your family."

In a somber tone, Lila replied, "Me, too."

The drive on the way home was one big blur. The entire time, Lila prayed that her mom had not yet heard the news. She pulled up just in time to find her mom pulling into the driveway at the same time.

"Hi Mom, is everything alright?" Lila asked. She could see that Marie's pale skin was beet red and her eyes were swollen from crying.

"Yes, Lila, everything's *fine*. Why aren't you at work?" Marie asked as she stumbled out of the car. "I forgot to get my favorite blanket. I was heading to the beach and realized that my blanket was not in the car. I have to find it."

Lila could see an empty bottle of wine in the back seat through the car window. Marie staggered towards the door, and Lila's stance was prepared to catch her in case she fell. An eerie cold chill ran down her spine as she listened to her mother's slurred speech. "Lila, what are you doing here?" Marie asked, but Lila did not answer. Standing at the front door of the house, she watched her mother fumble with the wrong key as she tried to put it into the keyhole.

"Mom, let me help you." Lila took the keys from Marie and began to open the door. Lila walked in ahead of Marie and saw the blanket hanging off the arm of the couch in the living room. She grabbed it. "I found it! I think I'll go with you if that's okay. I have nothing to do, and I have the rest of the day off." Her words were met with silence. "Mom?" Lila looked around. The house was quiet, and there was no sign of Marie.

Suddenly, the sound of profuse vomiting could be heard coming from the bathroom. "Mom!" Lila dropped everything and ran to the bathroom, only to find Marie passed out in her own vomit. "What is happening? Mom, what were you drinking?" The smell of an unknown, yet familiar chemical filled the room. "Mom, wake up! I need to know what you've been drinking." At that moment, Lila looked over at the bathroom sink and saw an empty bottle of Liquid Drain-O. She picked up the bottle and smelled it. "Oh, God, no! NO, NO, NO!" Lila rolled Marie onto her side and ran to the phone to call 911.

It felt like just a few seconds had passed between the time Lila called 911 and the arrival of the ambulance. Marie was unconscious and Lila had been frantically trying to wake her until they arrived. For the first time, the little girl in Lila was desperate not to lose her mommy. Memories of Lila and her mom danced across the screen of her mind as she cried out to God in disbelief and desperation. "God, I don't understand what is happening here, but I know You know all things. Please spare us from the tragedy of losing my mom. Give her another chance!" Lila rode in the ambulance with Marie, clutching her hand the entire time crying, "Come back to me, Mommy. Please, come back to me."

Later that night, Lila stood in shock as the doctor told her how they had to pump half of a gallon of drain cleaner from her mother's stomach. In an instant, Lila realized that Marie had not been planning to return from her trip to the beach; she had planned to lay on her blanket, watch the sunset, and drift off into an endless sleep, where there would be an end to her pain.

"Mom, what were you thinking?" Lila whispered as she leaned gently over the side of the hospital bed, not realizing that her mother had regained consciousness.

A tear ran down Marie's cheek as she turned her face to the wall and quietly said, "Lila, unless you've ever been in love, I don't expect you to understand."

"Mom, what does that mean? Can we start from the beginning, please?"

Marie let out a sigh and knew that Lila was not going to leave until she knew the details of her love affair. She felt as if she owed Lila the truth for imposing such a traumatic experience on her baby girl. She knew that Lila could never unsee what she had witnessed that day. Marie was now guilty of inflicting trauma on her own child. She was becoming the mother she had always feared she would become: a defective, faulty, negligent and careless one. The mother she never wanted to be like, was her own.

Without hesitation, she began. "Richard and I were going to get married, Lila."

"Mom, how could you marry Mr. Clemmons when you are still married to Dad?"

"I filed for divorce some time ago, Lila, and it's almost finalized. I'm just waiting for the final documents to come in the mail." Lila stared at her mom with a look of bewilderment as Marie continued. "I spoke with Richard this morning, and he said that he was fed up and tired of arguing with his wife, Shelly. He mentioned that he could not wait to be with me, because I am the only one who understands him.

He called me his 'one and only queen,' and I desperately wanted to believe him. He knew how to pour his love upon me in a way that your father never could. I loved how he loved me, and how he made me feel. With Richard, I felt free. He gave me the permission that I needed to freely be myself, and I was no longer invisible. And he loved me, just as I am. I don't believe that it was your father's intention, but he always made me feel like I was inadequate. All I wanted from your father was to be seen..." Marie paused, as though deep in thought. "Richard said that it wouldn't be much longer before we would be together, and I believed him. I'm not sure what happened between six o'clock this morning, which was the time we last spoke, and the time he took his own life, but when I got the news, my heart shattered into a thousand pieces. I just..." breathing heavily, Marie paused before finding the strength to continue. "I just couldn't go on living." Marie lay in a pool of her own tears.

"Mom, did you ever stop and think for a moment about how we might feel about losing you? If Troy would not have called me at work, or if you would not have come back home to get your blanket, you would not be alive right now." Lila's heart broke at the thought, and the dam that held back her tears broke with it.

"I'm so sorry, baby," Marie said, failing at her attempt to comfort her only daughter. "I realize that my own grief has brought you agony. I was consumed by my own heartache, and I am so sorry for bringing this upon you."

Lila looked up at her mom and said with a tender voice and a face wet with tears, "Mom, if the man you loved could murder his wife of 20 some odd years, what would have stopped him from killing you?"

CHAPTER 8

Conversations with Mama

"As a fair exchange–I speak as to my children–
open wide your hearts also."
2 Corinthians 6:13 (NIV)

Present Day

One of my favorite things about Mama is that she has always been *so* easy to talk to. Growing up, and all throughout high school, I could tell my Mama anything – and I do mean *anything*. We talked about the things that most daughters would be afraid to tell their moms, especially things that would get them into trouble. I think Mama loved listening to me talk about everything that was going on in my life as much as I loved sharing the details about them. She also loved talking to me as much as I loved listening. By the time I turned 14, we were growing up together and became the best of friends. We were two peas in a pod. In fact, most of the men who found my Mama attractive thought I was her sister. Imagine that!

Mama often tells me the story about the first time she allowed Lula to babysit me for the weekend. I was about four months old, and Lula had convinced Mama to take the weekend to rest and pamper herself. Though Mama seemed apprehensive, she finally agreed, saying, "My time was consumed with being a full-time single parent, and I needed a break!" Mama had no problem sharing. Well, as Mama tells it, that only lasted about an hour.

"I stood in the middle of the street, watching the car drive away until it reached the stop sign. As soon as you two disappeared from my sight, I began to cry. I hollered, 'Come back!'" Mama recalled through teary-eyed laughter. Then she continued, "I waited about an hour then said, 'Nope! I can't do it!' So, I hopped in my car and headed to Torrance, California where Lula was staying at the time. I knocked on her front door and said, 'I've decided that I'm going to come and spend a little time over here with the two of you.'" Then, Mama would switch into her Lula voice as she told the story. "Lila, do you think that I'm NOT going to bring her back?" Mama theatrically began to imitate herself. "I said, 'Look here, Marie. This here is *my* child, and I just can't stand to be away from her yet.'" As Mama tells it, my Lula let out a long sigh before letting her come in. Mama tells this story so well, that I often forget that it is a story she shared with me, rather than a memory of my own making. After all, I was only four months old when it happened.

Mama could not stand to be away from me, as much as I could not stand to be away from her. I would even dare to say that we both suffered from separation anxiety. When it was time for Mama to return to work, my Great Grammy K took care of me. I was only six months old at the time, and I was a breastfed baby who refused to take a bottle, so I gave my Grammy K hell. Mama told me that I cried all day until it was time for her to come to my rescue.

Grammy K was a praying woman. She would cover me with her prayers and take me with her to church. When I was about four years old, my Grammy K took me to a Sunday morning church service. The church was packed and the congregation full. Before we arrived, Grammy K had asked if I wanted to get baptized. Like a good girl, I sweetly replied, "Yes." My Grammy K would soon find out that I had no idea what she was talking about, and I was too young at the time to admit it.

During the morning service, the congregation clapped their hands and filled the air with shouts of Amen and Hallelujah. The Preacher preached and the sweet melodies that the choir sang warmed my young soul. Grammy K held my hand as we walked towards the front of the church during the altar call. She told the tall Preacher man who held a microphone in his hand that I wanted to be baptized. The large man who appeared tall enough to reach the ceiling held everyone at attention. It seemed that all eyes were on him, or maybe they were on me.

He leaned down and spoke with a voice so soft, it did not match his appearance. "Do you believe that the Lord Jesus Christ died on the cross and rose again for your sins?"

I looked up at the kindhearted man and answered most assuredly, "No!"

The whole congregation gasped, but the man never flinched. He shared with me that Jesus Christ loved me so much that He died to take away my sins. He explained that we all were born sinners and that it is the nature of humankind to sin.

"We all need the Savior," he said, "and that savior is Jesus Christ."

I did not know what to say. I was only four years old, and I only wanted to please Grammy K. Something felt right about that moment. I felt safe, so I replied, "Okay!"

They walked me to a room behind the altar where a change of clothes awaited me. Grammy K helped me get dressed and led me to a large tub of water. The water inside was warm. The nice man, who was no longer holding his microphone, waited for me in the water. He asked me again, "Do you believe that the Lord Jesus Christ died for your sins and rose again so that you may live?"

This time I replied, "Yes!"

The kind man smiled. I held my breath and let the man, whom I now trusted, lean me back into the water, which fully engulfed me. That was the day that I was baptized – for the first time. It would not be long before the time would come, when I recognized my own sinful state, and would feel the need for my sins to be washed away… again.

CHAPTER 9

Shattered Hope

The LORD is close to the brokenhearted;
he rescues those whose spirits are crushed.

Psalm 34:18 (NLT)

May of 1984

I was six months old when my biological father came to meet me for the first time.

"Hello, Lila!" the man's voice cheerily said when Mama answered the phone. She was surprised to hear his voice on the other end.

"Hello." Mama's response was serene, as she hoped her heart would not betray her. Although her voice and exterior were calm, her insides screamed unmentionable words, like *Where the bleep, bleep have you been? What kind of man takes six months to decide if he's going to be a father or not? What a bleeping fool I must be to even entertain a conversation with you!* She felt her heart begin to race, and her emotions birthed a tear that gently rolled down her cheek. His call was unexpected but not unwanted. Mama sat in confusion and inner turmoil wondering why she longed to see the man who had abandoned her and her precious baby girl.

"Lila, are you there?" He waited for her to reply.

"What do you want?" is all she could manage to say.

"I know you're mad at me, but I'd like an opportunity to explain. I would like to meet the baby –"

"Zoe," Lila interrupted. "Her name is Zoe!" She wanted to cry, knowing that the father of her child did not even know the name of his own daughter.

After much deliberation and reluctance, she agreed to meet with him for dinner, but it was strictly to discuss Zoe and make arrangements for visitation. She swore that it would not matter how fine he looked or how sweet his words were; she would not allow her heart to beat for him again... ever!

The man she once loved but now despised met her at the finest restaurant he had ever taken her to, and he had already taken her to many. Mama went dressed like she had just left a photo shoot for *Ebony Magazine*. He could not take his eyes off her. She wore a chic, black-and-white striped dress that hugged her model-like figure. The dress framed her curves in all the right places. Looking at her head-on, the halter top of the elegant dress embraced the lower curve of her slender neck, while the back of the dress opened into a seductive V shape that accentuated her tail bone. She stood an inch shorter than him in her black-and-white stiletto heels, and her vanilla skin glowed in the moonlight.

He kissed her delicately on the hand. "Lila, I've missed you so much." She wanted so badly to believe him but thought if it were true, it would not have taken six months for him to finally introduce himself to his daughter. *I should be disgusted with you, so, why aren't I? Why didn't you tell me you were married? What about this son I hear you have? You're a liar and a cheat*, was the song Lila sang in her inner voice. *Why am I even here?* Lila brushed away her thoughts, as though they were an annoying fly. Her handsome date held her hand as the waiter escorted them to their table.

The romantic ambiance of the restaurant, coupled with the delicious dish, made her close her eyes and moan with every bite. Looking into his eyes and inhaling his essence sent chills up and down her spine. *Lila, guard your heart!* she heard a small voice inside call out to her. Looking across the table, Lila knew that she needed to protect her heart, but just one look at him made her want to fall... again.

Dinner was amazing. Afterwards, the father of her child made plans to take her to a movie. "Do you mind if I make a quick stop at my cousin's house first?" he asked. "I owe him some money and he's hounding me for it."

"Sure," she responded.

"Great! It will only take a minute," he assured her. There was something in that last phrase that told Lila that it would be more than *just* a minute.

They made their way across town. The lights on each block seemed to grow dimmer as they entered into a questionable part of town, and pulled up to what looked like a deserted house. Bars covered every window, and it did not look like anyone was home. Suddenly, her stomach was upset. The house was reminiscent of the crack houses that she would frequent in the past. He opened the car door for her, but everything in her told her to stay put. He took her by the hand and repeated the words, "It will only take a minute." She shuttered at his words but chose to trust him.

Together, they walked up to the door of the house, and before he could knock on the door, a voice shouted, "It's open!"

They walked inside, and he bolted the door behind them. There were two men who greeted him like they were long-lost friends. They looked at Lila like she was a piece of prime rib waiting to be devoured. Her date made himself comfortable on the couch while she continued to stand.

"Would you like something to drink?" one of the men asked, staring at her ravenously.

"Uh, no thank you. We just ate, and we will be leaving soon," Lila replied. She gave her date a "Hurry up" look, but he did not seem to understand her rush.

"Man, you are *wearing* that dress!" the other wolf-like man said as he entered the living room from the kitchen, clutching a small pouch in his hand.

Lila felt surrounded. She was defenseless. The men sat down and looked as though they were in anticipation of whatever was in that pouch. The ravenous one began pulling out small rocks, one at a time.

"I'm ready to go," Lila said, when she realized what the tiny rocks were. She had lived sober for more than six months and was determined to resist the pull of temptation.

Her sub-par hero date looked at her and said, "We will in a minute. The guys just want to have a little fun."

Just then, she realized that her marvelously wonderful date had become a nightmare. She was being set up. He had no intention of taking her to the movies. There was no movie.

The men began chopping up the rocks into tiny pieces until the rocks eventually became like dust. One by one, the men took turns sniffing it up into their nostrils.

"I'm ready to go!" Lila said impatiently. No one responded. She was still standing, and her feet were beginning to ache from the six-inch heels she wore for her date.

One of the men stood up from the couch and staggered his way towards her. She noticed that his pants were unbuttoned. Lila started backing up and heading to the door, which had been deadbolted from the inside.

"Look, this will be a lot easier if you participate." The words of the man she trusted pierced her heart. Hopeless and trapped, she picked up the tray of cocaine and started snorting line after line in order to make the bad dream go away. The room grew dim, the voices of men faded in the darkness, and her fear subsided as the coke flooded her veins.

Lila woke up to her dress pulled up above her chest and her bra removed. The three men were groping her, and one was on top, trying to enter into her delicate parts. She was too intoxicated to respond with words, so she cried. She tried to move her arms, but they felt like they weighed a ton. All she could do was shake her head back and forth as if to say, "NO!"

The ravenous man began to rush the man on top of her. "Man, I can't get it up! I shouldn't have hit that last line."

The wolf-like man let out a howling laugh, while pushing his counterpart off of her. He began making his way on top while trying to arouse an erection. The cocaine had made both men impotent. At last, the man whom she loved and had hoped to wed came near, as though he knew he would be the victor in this competition. He picked her up, threw her limp body against the wall, and began to have his way with her as the other men sat and watched in defeat.

It was raining and there was gross darkness outside. As the drops of rain fell on her cold, limp body, she wished she could lay there and allow the rain to wash the filth away from her body and soul.

"Lila, get in. I'm taking you to your car," he said coldly.

The man Lila had once loved threw her into the car, as if she were trash to be discarded. Drifting in and out of consciousness, Lila woke up to the sound of a car door shutting. The man she once loved had left her in her car, alone and abandoned.

Lila's heart and mind raced as the fear that departed returned so soon. She managed to stick the key into the ignition and turn on the windshield wipers. She could not see out of the window; not due to the rain outside, but the tears that filled her eyes. She glanced over at the clock. Although she was unable to focus clearly, she managed to read 3:03 AM. All Lila wanted was to get home, but she was in no condition to drive. She started up her car and paused, wondering where she would go. *I can't go to my mom's like this. My baby may see me,* Lila thought. Her hair was in shambles and her mascara ran along her cheeks and had stained her beautiful dress. Worst of all, she reeked with the odor of polluted men and semen. The only place to go was to her brother Robert's house, if she could only get there in one piece. She decided to take a chance.

Driving in the unrelenting rain felt like a death sentence to Lila. Her mind flooded with questions of *Why? Why would he do this to me? What did I do to deserve this? Why would he lie to me and leave me out here to die? Doesn't he care that I am the mother of his child? God, why would You let this happen to me?*

In an instant, Lila's car began to spin out of control down the slippery road. With a terrified and desperate scream, Lila exhaled all of the breath from her lungs, but the screeching sound of the tires drowned out the sound of her cry. For a brief moment, Lila welcomed death. The car came to an abrupt halt in the middle of the street. Coincidentally, there were no cars, and no one was around; it was just Lila and God. Sobbing with her face buried in her hands, Lila cried the only words she had strength enough to utter. "Heavenly

Father, please help me." Putting the car back in drive, she took a deep breath and began to make her way to her brother's house. As she drove, she thought, *not once did he ask about his newborn daughter.*

"What the hell happened to you, Lila?"

She entered her brother Robert's house trying not to cry so loud as to wake his sleeping wife and kids. Lila told her eldest brother the entire agonizing story from start to finish. Robert managed not to throw a chair against the wall in his fury. Instead, he cussed under his breath and threw deadly punches at an invisible man.

"I knew something was wrong when Mom called at two in the morning asking if I had heard from you. She tried to sound calm, but I could hear the panic in her voice and the baby crying in the background."

Lila bowed her head into her lap and cried. "I can't be a mother, Robert. You, Mom and Dad were right. I should have listened to you when you told me to get an abortion. Zoe would have been better off dying in my womb than living with me as her mother."

"Don't *ever* say that again, Lila - *ever*!" Robert's tone spoke with the authority of a father. "Parents aren't perfect! Hell, I'm not a perfect dad. But we do the best we can in hopes that our children will glean the good from our lives and resist the temptation to hoard the bad."

"But how could I let this happen, Robert? If I can't protect myself, how am I supposed to keep Zoe safe?" Lila's once-beautiful dress became drenched with tears as she realized that the road to recovery and victory over cocaine that she previously traveled, had now taken a turn toward despair and defeat.

"Lila, we have to get you help. But first, let's get you cleaned up. Then, we need to call Mom and check on Zoe."

Lila took a shower and borrowed some of her sister-in-law's clothes. She rested in the quietness of the living room on her brother's couch but could not sleep. The sun rose and offered the hope of a new day, yet Lila did not think that the offer extended to her. During the phone call with her mother, Lila recounted the prior evening's events, selectively choosing details that she knew would not send her mother over the edge. The response from her mother, however, consisted of Marie yelling at her for what felt like half an hour. Marie was furious when she discovered that Lila went on a date with a married man, let alone the same man who abandoned her child, and could not understand why Lila had not called sooner, if for nothing more than to check on her six-month-old daughter, who had stayed up all night crying for her mommy's milk.

"Mama, the only reason that I agreed to the date was because we were supposed to talk about scheduling a time for him to visit Zoe on a regular basis. He told me that he wanted to see Zoe and become a part of her life." Lila left out the part about him wanting to talk about being a couple and that not once did he even mention Zoe.

Lila apologized for not calling to check on Zoe and told her mother that she was checking herself into the local rehabilitation center. She knew that her body was already craving another hit to mask the pain, and she also knew just where to find one. Lila was aware that if she did not seek help now to treat her trauma, she would never be whole for herself or her daughter.

"Robert is going to take me, Mama. I will make sure that I call as soon as I get the opportunity. Please kiss Zoe for me. I'm doing this for her."

"I will, Lila," Marie replied.

"Thank you, Mama. Goodbye."

As Lila went to hang up the phone, she heard her mother call out to her. "Lila?"

"Yes, Mama."

"I love you." Click.

CHAPTER 10

The Only Man I've Ever Called Daddy

Love must be sincere…

Romans 12:9a (BSB)

The Summer of 1988

"Knock, knock!" I said in my five-year-old voice, as I knocked on the bathroom door. "Mama, can I come in?"

Mama replied with irritation, "Yes, Zoe."

I entered the bathroom with caution and sat my tiny bottom on the toilet, feet dangling back and forth. As I sat there, I noticed that something was different. Mama never closed the decorative sheer curtain before while taking a bath, but today, it was stretched along the tub, obscuring her from my clear view. My little mind began to race as I washed my hands and dried them.

"Mama, are you pregnant?" is all I thought to ask. I was shocked as much as Mama at the choice of my own words. How would I even know what pregnancy was at the tender age of five? I could see Mama look at me with wide eyes filled with shock through the light blue floral curtain.

"Yes, Zoe! Now, get out!" Mama shouted.

I almost leaped out of my skin as I shut the door behind myself. Unsure if I should be wounded from my mother's harsh tone, I stood at the bathroom door with the biggest smile on my face. I was going to be a big sister! It felt as if only seconds had passed while I waited for Mama to come out. She opened the door wrapped in a bath towel and walked right past me as though I were invisible.

"Mama, can I have a little sister?" I asked in my excitement. She turned around and looked at me, this time with a soft look in her eyes. Mama did not answer. Instead, she cupped my chin in her hand and kissed my forehead. I thought that this would be an ideal time to eagerly put in another request.

"Well, if it is a boy, can you send it back?"

Mama giggled and said, "I don't think that it works that way, Zoe."

As she walked away and glanced at me from over her shoulder, I silently thought, *Well, why not?*

Mama met Daddy when I was two-and-a-half years old. There were no fuzzy feelings and no butterflies upon her initial introduction to him, just a business card with his name on it. He had asked his older sister to pass it along the day he laid eyes on Mama at my babysitter's house. He had a son named Kenneth who was a year older than I; our birthdays were just a few days apart. Kenneth and I became friends while our parents became lovers. The couple started off slowly with a few dinner dates here and there, which eventually evolved into trips to Buena Vista Lake where he taught Mama how to jet ski. Soon after, Mama was invited to an exclusive, members-only fraternity party, where they dressed in all white and were the flyest couple there. All of Daddy's frat brothers wanted to know who the breathtaking lady was who joined him.

"She's mine! We brotha's and all, but go near her and..." He did not have to finish his sentence. They knew what he meant. Mama was strikingly beautiful, and in every way imaginable, she was lovely. Daddy stood six foot three inches tall with a smooth caramel skin tone. He wore a neatly groomed goatee and always dressed to impress. Daddy was sleek and slim with a toned muscle build, and everywhere he went, someone always seemed to know him by name; I thought he was famous! By the time the two became a couple, Mama had achieved two years of sobriety and was proud to be sober and clean. She felt new, looked polished and all her scars had healed. Daddy treated her like royalty. He loved to purchase the flyest clothing for her, just so he could see how glamorous she looked in them.

Being with Daddy made me feel safe. He called me his daughter every time he introduced me to someone new. I was the daughter who finally belonged. He would pick me up by my little four-year-old arms and lift me high above his head to place me on his shoulders. I loved being with my Daddy. He never ignored me, was never ashamed of me, and made sure I knew exactly what I meant to him. Within just a few months of them dating, I loved my Daddy.

Daddy was a businessman who owned his own construction company. He was hardworking and took pride in everything his hands touched. He would often take me with him on business trips to pay visits to the workers at his construction sites. The workers were so nice. Everyone looked up to Daddy, and he always showed them respect. I was his princess, and he wanted the world to know.

The day I found out that Mama was pregnant was the happiest day of my life! I wanted a little sister *so* badly. Daddy had bought us a house to live in, and it was a nice one. We lived in a city called Long Beach, and my new brother Kenneth and I loved to ride our bikes down the street to the park. We grew pretty close, and I officially had myself a big brother. We climbed trees, played cops and robbers while shooting each other with cap guns and enjoyed eating free meals at the park during the summers. We were aces.

Daddy had been around for roughly over a year now, and he didn't seem to have any plans of leaving. Mama was engaged for the second time in her life. However, this time, it was more than a promise made with words; she was given a beautiful ring. Unlike me, my little sister would know her father.

Mama's stomach was nice and round. Sissy covered every inch of her belly. Although there was no way for Mama to know, I knew it was a girl and that she would be born any day now. Mama never wanted me to get my hopes up and everything seemed perfect - until things suddenly changed.

"Lila, my frat brother is coming over this afternoon," Daddy mentioned as Mama walked out the door.

"That's fine. I'll be right back. I'm dropping Zoe off at my mom's house for the weekend. Will Kenneth be coming over?" Mama asked.

"No, he's with his mom this weekend, so I get to have you all to myself."

Mama blushed. "And what do you expect to do with all this belly?" she questioned.

"You'll see! I've been known to work miracles!" Daddy said with assurance as Mama smiled and walked out the door.

In anticipation of a romantic evening with her fiancé, Mama dropped me off, kissed Lula on the cheek, and rushed to the nearest grocery store to pick up a few items. As she walked down each aisle with joy, she thought of the most delicious meal that she could create that would speak the language of love. A lobster tail for her love, a Cornish hen for herself and the baby, asparagus, and petite potatoes with fresh rosemary for roasting. For dessert, she would bake her famous German chocolate cake and top it off with a scoop of vanilla bean ice cream. She could not wait! In her excitement, she almost forgot that she was pregnant, as she moved faster than a group of teenage girls on their way to a Boyz II Men concert.

Mama pulled up in the driveway, only to discover a car parked in her spot. She did not recognize the car, but she remembered that her love had mentioned having company this afternoon.

Great! Mama thought. *This gives me the perfect opportunity to keep dinner a surprise.* Shaking off the urge to be upset about her parking space being stolen; she unloaded her groceries and carried them into the house. As she turned the key and pushed open the front door, the sight that greeted her made her heart sink into the pit of her stomach. *Not this again!* she thought.

Lila almost dropped her groceries as she entered the house. She fought back the impulse to curse the unknown man who was snorting crack in her living room and tell him to get the bleep, bleep out of her house. Her love just sat there like this was a norm and was to be expected.

"Baby, this is my frat brother that I was telling you about, Jeremy." Her love tried to not notice her discomfort.

Lila rolled her eyes and walked straight through the living room and into the kitchen without saying a word. Angry and disgusted, she no longer had the desire to prepare a romantic meal. She threw the food into the fridge, literally. *What a waste of a good evening,* Lila thought. She sat at the kitchen table with her hands covering her face and cried. After a few minutes, Lila began to ask herself why she was so angry. After all, she knew that her fiancé had had a previous relationship with her nemesis, cocaine. He had never kept their relationship, or the fact that he had a few friends that also took interest in his mistress a secret. So, why did she feel so enraged? With a heart full of sorrow, she realized the real source of her anger: her lust for the white dust still had its hold on her. Lila felt envious of the two men, as they enjoyed the company of her former lover, cocaine. She thought that it was over between them. It had been two whole years since she had been in the presence of the powder. Now, suddenly, it was in her house, having its way with her man, on her couch. Worst of all, Lila had to fight the urge to go into the living room and join them.

Lila decided to go ahead and prepare her meal, knowing that it would keep her mind occupied and her hands busy. She needed this distraction, as she could not afford to place herself or her baby in the unpredictable hands of the white powder. Before long, the kitchen was smelling good. After nearly an hour had passed, Lila thought, *Maybe I should go out there and check on them*. She entered the living room hesitantly, cautiously approaching as if a monster would pop out of nowhere at any given second. The two men were on the couch sitting still, like zombies.

"Hey, baby!" her fiancé called out. "It's smelling good in there. You cookin' for me, baby?"

Mama nodded her head, having flashbacks of her last encounter with men and cocaine. She cried silent tears.

"Baby, what's the matter? Is everything okay?" he asked.

Mama stood at the doorway reliving that dark day. Vivid memories roamed through her head; memories of the day that she had wanted to die. Her fiancé had always made her feel safeguarded against her cocaine addiction, the enemy of her soul, but not on this day. This day, she knew that she was in danger all over again.

"Baby, come here," her fiancé said, as he sat straight up from his seat and beckoned her to come. Slowly, she walked up to him. He kissed her belly. His warmth brought her soul comfort. He gently pulled her down onto his lap, cradling and engulfing her with all of his love.

Lila sat on her fiancé's lap and watched television as he drifted off to sleep. Jeremy stood up and yawned while taking a long, good stretch. He looked Lila in the eye then said, "Lila, it's been a pleasure to meet you." He gave a wave as he escorted himself out of the door. Lila's eyes followed him until the door shut. She scanned the table that sat in front of the spot he'd occupied on the sofa. There was one more line left on the little black tray. She looked at it, then back at her love. "No," she said aloud, as if there were someone there to hear her.

Lila tried flipping through the channels on the television to find something that met her interest. There was nothing. She looked at her love, who was sleeping soundly, again. *It won't hurt to take one hit and then relax in the arms of my love*, she thought, only to discover that she was wrong. That one hit incited her body to want more. In that moment, Lila forgot about the unborn child she carried, and like an itching fiend, she rummaged frantically through her fiancé's pants pockets looking for another rock. She found none. Lila sat for a minute, thinking about where she could go to buy some more.

It only took a moment for her to spark a plan of action of how to fulfill the craving that now raged inside of her. That one moment would send Lila spiraling out of control; lost again in her addiction. Her fiancé would not find out until the next morning that Lila had taken the keys to his car and all the money from his wallet in order to reunite with her old lover, cocaine. She went down familiar roads, knocking on the door of old familiar crack houses, until one finally opened the door.

"Lila, what the hell are you doing here?" the man behind the door asked as he stood peering at her through a crack in the door. "As I recall, the last time you came around here, you made me promise not to let you come in. Besides, look at you," he said, his eyes scanning her up and down, giving her a once over until they reached her full, round belly. The tall, husky man looked like he could bench press a car, and yet he spoke with the tenderness of a friend.

"What is that supposed to mean?" Lila asked, feeling irritated. She only wanted what she'd come for, not a lecture.

"Look at you, Lila! You look like you are about to burst. Now, get out of here before you have that baby on my front porch!" The husky man pleaded.

"I'm not leaving here until I get what I came for!" Lila shouted.

"Damn, girl! Be quiet before you wake my neighbors." After gesturing for her to wait, the gentle giant walked away from the door, disappearing from Lila's sight. Lila tried to peek through the cracked door to ensure that he wasn't up to any funny business. After a few minutes, he returned and handed Lila a small pouch. When Lila reached over to hand him the cash, her hand brushed his, and he held onto it, looking her directly in the eyes.

"Lila," he began, with a serious look on his face, "you've been my girl since high school. You know that I have always gotten you whatever you needed. I'm about to say this because I care about you and that baby in your belly." He paused before continuing with a deep, stern voice. "Don't *ever* come back here again. You know how good I am in keeping my promises? Well, I'm even better in fulfilling my threats." The sound of the door slamming made Lila jump. Lila quickly ran back to the car and started it up, still startled by the fear of the gentle giant's threat. After driving back to her house, Lila did not get out of the car. Instead, she sat there in the driver's seat and crushed the rocks into dust. With frenzy she sniffed the powder into her nostrils, rekindling her toxic relationship with cocaine once more. After taking the hit, she slumped over in the front seat with the feeling of being cradled in the arms of her long-lost abusive lover. A single solitary tear ran down her cheekbone. The pleasure she sought while fulfilling her craving was met with consuming regret as she drifted off into a deep, teary-eyed sleep.

Knock, Knock, Knock! Lila woke up to a loud, aggressive knock on the car window.

"Lila, what the hell are you doing sleeping in the car?" a bewildered voice called out through the glass, irritating her as it roused her from her sleep. It was morning, and the bright sunshine made it difficult for Lila to open her eyes and see who was speaking, though she recognized the voice of her fiancé. He was not a welcomed sight. Lila was angry at her fiancé for not protecting her from the demon that had plagued her life since high school. She felt like a victim to the narcotic and wondered if this vicious cycle would ever end for her. As Lila slowly opened the door and inched her way out of the car, the father of her baby tried to assist her. Lila refused his help.

"Leave me alone," Lila groaned as she walked past him, leaving him standing in the driveway with questions swirling around in his head.

Their relationship was never quite the same after that. Lila was not the same either. Here she was due any day, and yet reliving the same pain of her past. She was overcome with grief yet again. Shame consumed her, and she found herself traveling down the dark and dreary road to depression. On a downward spiral she went, constantly looking for just one more hit until the day a stabbing pain in her womb shocked her back into reality.

"What am I doing?" Lila asked aloud to an invisible presence as she sat on the floor in her bathroom. There was no answer. "I'm tired, God. God, I'm so tired," she sobbed. Her cry echoed, but there was no one home to hear or comfort her. Looking down at the rocks in her hand, she felt the sharp, piercing pain in her stomach again. However, the pain this time was so fierce that it was as though the tiny person in her womb was crying out to her, *enough!* Lila looked up and saw the phone sitting on the counter of the bathroom sink. She knew what she had to do. In a moment of surrender, she reached over, picked up the phone and began to dial a number she knew by heart.

"Hello. Thank you for calling Westminster Rehabilitation Center. How may we serve you today?" a kind voice asked.

A desperate Lila responded, "Hi, my name is Lila Rene Love, and I would like to check myself in tonight."

The tender voice on the other end said, "I'm sorry, honey, but we are completely booked. If you try calling back in a few months, we may have some room available then. Again, I am terribly sorry."

Lila held her breath. Where would she go, if not to rehab? The answer scared her because it was clear: to the nearest dope dealer. Fearful at the thought, Lila exclaimed, "Ma'am, if you don't take me, I am going to kill myself and my baby!"

The startled receptionist blurted out, "Oh, no! We will take you right now! Please, come right away and we will make room for you."

Lila tried to stand up, although she felt weak and frail. She looked in the mirror. The person staring back at her seemed unrecognizable. "What happened to you Lila? How did we get here again?" She asked the woman looking back at her. Just then, Lila could hear the front door shutting. She glanced at the clock and realized that the whole day had gone by. Her fiancé had just arrived from work and picking up Zoe and Kenny from school. Lila hurriedly splashed water on her face in hopes that the warm water would mask her sorrow. Entering into the bedroom, Lila would not pack a bag for her time away; she would go to rehab with only the clothes on her back. She only packed for Zoe Maree, who would be spending the next six weeks with Uncle Troy.

"You're going somewhere?" her fiancé asked in a tone that seemed more like a statement than a question. He watched her as she busily moved around and got Zoe's things together.

"Just for a little while. But I must go now, or I'll be late," she replied.

"Lila, what's going on? Did I do something? Where are you going?" Her fiancé's voice now seemed filled with concern.

"Please, no more questions. I will tell you everything soon." Lila knew that her fiancé would be fine on his own for the six weeks of rehab she would embark upon in order to regain her life. For now, she had to put herself, Zoe and their unborn baby first.

"Lila, are you okay?" Her fiancé asked, with a concerned look on his face.

"No." Lila paused briefly. "No, I'm not." It hurt Lila to admit the truth. She hugged her love while kissing him softly, then took Zoe by the hand and walked out the door.

I still recall Mama taking me on the long drive up the 110 Freeway to live with Uncle Troy. I sat in the front seat of her '72 Chevy Nova, bouncing up and down as we drove along the freeway. I looked over at Mama and could see that she was troubled. She wasn't crying, but her face looked as though she were in pain. I glanced at her belly which almost reached the steering wheel, making it difficult for her to make sharp turns. When we arrived, Uncle Troy was waiting for us on the front porch. I ran and jumped into his arms. He smelled of hot chocolate, and kissed my cheek, then put me back down to hug Mama.

"Come in," he said, as he motioned to Mama.

"No, I have to go now, or I may lose my spot."

I was only five years old, so I did not understand what the concerned look on his face meant. He nodded his head in agreement. Mama handed him my bag then turned and headed back toward the car. Uncle Troy looked down at me. He smiled before scooping me up into his arms, carried me into the house, and shut the door.

We watched out of the front window as my Mama drove away, leaving me behind. A feeling of dread came over me as I realized; I didn't even get to say goodbye.

CHAPTER 11

Dwelling Place

Then may You hear from heaven, Your dwelling place,
their prayer and petition, and may You uphold their cause.

I Kings 8:49 (BSB)

At the tender age of six, children usually run around without a care in the world. Little feet pitter-patter down hallways, as tiny giggling voices follow. Bright smiles fill their faces from ear to ear, their little hearts are filled with love, and their tiny arms are full of tender hugs. At this age, they love kisses and are not ashamed to hold on to Mommy and Daddy's hands while in public. This was my life during the time that I lived with my Uncle Troy. Life with him was vastly different than living with Mama. Uncle Troy provided safety and structure. I never had to worry about what time Uncle Troy would be home, or if I would be left in the dark alone, and there was always a delicious meal prepared for me during breakfast, lunch and dinner.

Mama never told me that I would be going to live with Uncle Troy, or why. The days turned into weeks and the weeks into months until finally, I wanted to stay with Uncle Troy forever... but good things never seemed to last long for me. During the first few weeks, I missed Mama, Daddy and Sissy. I missed hanging out with Kenneth and riding our bikes until the streetlights came on. I longed to go back to what was familiar. However, it became obvious that returning home was not going to be an option when Uncle Troy enrolled me at a new elementary school in the city of Altadena. That's when I decided to just enjoy the journey, because I would be staying for a while.

Uncle Troy is what I like to call a "creator." He has this gift of taking broken things and putting them back together better than they were before. He gets it from my Lula. His creative genius was always revealed in the dilapidated homes he would purchase. He would revive them and create a space that others would marvel at and want to stay in for long periods of time. He did the same thing with me, but I think that I am his best work.

Together, Uncle Troy and I loved to visit the United Artist movie theater in Old Town Pasadena. That was our spot. One day, on our journey to the theater, we bumped into a red-haired homeless man who sat outside playing his guitar for spare change. He looked as though he was lonely and felt invisible. Uncle Troy had a special way of making people feel seen. We stopped and gave him an opportunity to serenade us with his guitar, just before going into the theater. Uncle Troy and I applauded thunderously, as though we had just left the best concert we had ever attended. The bearded, red-haired homeless man smiled, as if to say we were the best audience he'd ever had the chance to play for in his open-air theater. As we walked away, Uncle Troy left the man a generous tip to show him just how much we appreciated that day's performance and looked forward to the next one during our next movie outing. I always wanted him to play just one more song as I looked over my tiny shoulder and gave him a wave goodbye. I did not view him as the vagrant that he was. In fact, oftentimes, I wanted Uncle Troy to allow us to take him home, so that he could be a part of our family.

On one of our father-daughter dates, we noticed that our favorite musician was a no-show. It seemed that Uncle Troy was as disappointed as I was. We had been looking forward to another one of the nice man's wondrous concerts, and until that day, our red-bearded friend had never seemed to disappoint. Uncle Troy tucked his cash back into his pocket as I looked frantically up and down the street, wondering where he might be. Worried and concerned, Uncle Troy held my hand and ushered me into the movie theater. There was a new guy standing at the door waiting to take our tickets. He had the same bright blue eyes as our friendly musician, and the same red hair, but this guy was polished and handsome, too. He smiled at me, and just then, I gasped in disbelief. I could recognize that smile anywhere. It was the same smile that our favorite musician wore. It was him! I looked up at Uncle Troy with wide eyes and mouth fully open, as if waiting for a fly to come in. I tugged at his coat and said, "Uncle Troy, look!"

"I know, Zoe," Uncle Troy replied, smiling back. "Let's not disturb him. He's working." I could not believe my little eyes. My heart felt joy and love for a stranger for the very first time in my little life.

It had been over a year since I had dwelt under the same roof as Mama and Daddy. My little Sissy was born beautiful and was as pretty as our Mama. Sissy's silky hair, vanilla skin and button nose made you think Mama had given birth to a miniature version of herself. Holding her and playing with her itty-bitty feet was the best part of my day.

One evening, Mama and Daddy went out on a date, leaving behind my big brother Kenneth and I with the babysitter. From my tiny perspective, the babysitter seemed to be no more than 16 or 17 years old. I don't remember her name or even her face. All I remember is her telling my brother and I was that we were about to play a game of hide and seek. I'm sure you can imagine the sheer joy that came across our little six and seven-year-old faces as we ran away to hide. I hid for what felt like hours, yet no one came to find me. I left my carefully picked hiding place and went in search of my brother. What I found left me standing in the doorway, petrified. The teenage babysitter was telling my brother to touch her in places that were forbidden. My eyes almost fell out of their sockets as I stood wanting to unsee what I had just seen.

When she realized that I was standing there in the doorway, the babysitter, who was supposed to be there to nurture and protect us, called me over to the bunk bed where they were. This is where it all began: the place where curiosity met with fear, although even still, I was more curious than I was afraid. It was that place where the little six-year-old girl inside of me prematurely evolved into a sexually driven teen. The place where the little girl would soon find herself losing her virginity at the vulnerable age of 12, growing up only to become a sexual object in the eyes of boys and men. I wandered into the place where my teenage heart would become more calloused with each new lover.

How does a little girl come to know the difference between love and lust when she never knew the pure, natural love that little girls receive from their biological fathers? Multiple daddies, but no father is her history and family legacy. Coupled with a constant lust for love and an insatiable need to be loved, this same little girl would become devoid of her purity and innocence. And this place… this place would become her new dwelling place.

Junior high was a whole new world for me. My innocence and untaintedness were replaced with a determination to avoid the reality that I was indeed, now tainted. This reality was kept a secret from others, and I avoided anyone who dared uncover the truth. By the time I reached the sixth grade, I was emotionally unavailable. Like a zombie, I walked around pretending to be fine, yet lifeless inside. Mama began to see the same destructive patterns within herself, now fully alive in me. Out of fear that I would turn out just like her, Mama sent me to live with Uncle Troy – again – although this time around, I was not the same Zoe Maree. I was just "Z." During the sixth grade, I was caught ditching class and my grades displayed my lack of enthusiasm towards education.

Uncle Troy sent me to a predominantly white middle school called "Pioneer" in Upland, California. All the boys thought I was cute, and the white girls wanted to know how my hair went from a short ponytail, to long flowing braids down the center of my back the next day. "Can I touch your hair?" one girl asked me, and before I could answer, she had her hands in my hair, tugging at my braids. I stood there with a blank stare on my face, irritated, but too kind to speak up.

While my physical body was at school, my mind was not, and my grades slowly began to reflect just that. When Uncle Troy received my report card, with disappointment he said, "Zoe, if you don't bring your grades up by the second semester, I am going to ship you back home to your Mama."

Back to *Mama*? How could he consider doing such a thing? When Mama wasn't at work, she was usually too busy entertaining her own demons to notice my darkness. Rehab didn't address the core of what made my Mama who she was; it only seemed to serve as a temporary fix, a bandage that would do its best to cover up the gaping wounds that riddled her heart. In light of this, if he truly loved me, why would Uncle Troy ever want to send me back there? Though I had known abandonment, I now felt rejected, like no one saw me or was willing to fight for what was best for me. Uncle Troy did not realize the magnitude of who he was and what he meant in my life. He didn't know that *he was* my home. He was my secret place of solace and my refuge. My safe haven. Yet, while I knew that Uncle Troy provided the stability I really needed, my flesh craved the freedom that Mama permitted.

In class, my secrets were my distraction. Dark thoughts caused me to lose the capacity to open my mind to receive what the teachers were teaching. My grades continued to decline, so back to Long Beach I went, leaving behind my secure dwelling place of consolation, and headed back down the crooked road to Freedom Ville.

CHAPTER 12

Freedom Ville

"My grace is all you need. My power works best in weakness."
2 Corinthians 12:9a (NLT)

I loved Freedom Ville; it was my favorite dwelling place. I likened it to a day in Las Vegas where what happens in Vegas, stays in Vegas. Since Mama worked long hours, I got to live my best life without adult supervision. Mama made the commute from Long Beach to Carson, California daily, giving me the liberty of walking to and from school. As an 11-year-old girl in the sixth grade, I loved the time spent walking home with friends and I loved the freedom that came with it even more.

Xavion was my first boyfriend, and I was infatuated with his exotic appearance. His caramel complexion and tight almond-shaped eyes made all the brown-skinned girls envy me. He wore his long-silky-brown hair in two cornrows with a zigzag part. He had a gentle-thug-look that made the fellas not want to step to him, yet his kind smile made them want to be his friend. One day, Xavion walked me home, so I invited him in to listen to music. I let him kiss me, and it wasn't long before we were lying on the floor in the hallway; the best location for keeping an ear towards the door. My skirt was raised, and he was trying to stick his private in me.

"Ouch!" I yelled. My cry caught us both off guard. Xavion was gentle, once he saw that I was in pain, he stopped and continued to kiss me instead. I appreciated his willingness in not pressuring me to continue. Little did I know, I was not ready to extend the invitation for another to inhabit my soul. Soon, I would discover that losing my virginity would open my soul to the world of perversion, tainting my purity even further.

A few weeks later, some friends of mine were hanging out after school, so I invited them to my place to just chill. We were in the living room drinking lemonade and playing music loudly when we heard a key turning in the door. We all stopped in our tracks and stared, hoping it was our imaginations. Just then, my mom walked in along with her boyfriend, Rodney. She had an "I'm about to beat your ass!" look on her face.

"Zoe, tell your friends goodbye. NOW!"

Petrified, my mouth said, "Goodbye," but in my head, I screamed, "Take me with you, *please*!"

To my surprise, Mama didn't spank me that day. Instead, she sent me to my room, but not before saying, "From now on, you will take the bus and the Metro Rail train to meet me at my job *every day* after school. As of this moment, you can't be trusted, Zoe."

As I sat on my bed, my heart filled with elation. I breathed in a deep sigh of relief as I thought to myself, *I'm just happy that you didn't come home early on the day that my boyfriend tried to stick his thing in me!*

The sun didn't shine too often in Freedom Ville. A cloud of distrust caused my mom to move me from one of the best middle schools in Long Beach, to what was, by far, the worst in Carson: Curtis Jr. High School. At Curtis, it felt like the only thing students learned was how the prison system worked. The air was filled with hatred and violence, and the teachers and staff were the prison guards. I had not been there any more than two weeks when I had my first fight. A girl in my third period class came up to me one day as we were leaving the classroom.

"You think you're cute," she said to me. "And since you think you're better than me, I'ma fu** you up!" she threatened.

"WHAT?" I replied, astonished.

I left that moment confused. *What would she think if she had actually entered my mind and caught a glimpse of my thoughts?* I wondered. Maybe then, she would have had sympathy for me, because she would be able to see all of my insecurities on full display. She would have seen that "cute" was the furthest thing I actually thought about myself.

That same week, the same girl came up behind me with her crew as we walked down the hallway, heading back to class from break. Without warning, she hit me in the back of the head. I thought that someone had just bumped into me until she and her friends pushed me to the ground and began to stomp the little dignity that I had left out of me. Looking back, I'm glad that I was on the ground. Little did they know that morning, I had brought a box cutter with me to school. I was so tired of girls threating me, that I'd put it in my pocket right before heading out the door for school. If I would have had access to the box cutter in my pocket, I might have taken someone's life that day, and the course of my life would have been forever altered by a potential conviction and relocation to juvenile hall.

A few weeks later, an ornery girl on the playground came up to me and said, "I am goin' to pluck your eyes out and put them on my teddy bear." I guess she liked the color of my hazel eyes and couldn't find a better way of saying it. I felt so fearful that I tried to hide in the girl's bathroom during our lunch break, but she followed me in there, too. This time around, before she could catch me off guard, I threw the first punch; I'd learned from my last experience not to let her push me to the ground. Then, I gave it all I had with each punch I threw. The teacher who caught us fighting sent us to the principal's office. When I explained to the principal how I'd felt threatened by her words, he gave me a pass, but he still suspended me for three days.

As is the protocol, they had to call my mom. I knew that Mama was going to be upset, because she had to leave work early – again, which meant that she was not making money, she was losing it; something a single mother could not afford to do. Mama entered the office with a look that was a blend of concern and frustration. "Not again, Zoe!" She said as she took her seat in the principal's office. I sat there silently as I listened to him describe his point of view about what had taken place with care.

"Miss Love, Zoe seems like a sweet girl, not at all like some of the girls we have here on campus. Though she has only been with us for a month and a half, I don't believe that she is provoking these fights." Mama felt sorry for me, turning her frustration into becoming my most trusted advocate. Upon leaving, Mama shook hands with the principal, and began planning my exit from the school.

From then on, the fear I possessed turned into paranoia. I wanted to attack anyone whom I thought might attack me first. A girl named Jennifer followed me home from school each day, and she kept talking trash to me because she knew that I had won my last fight and had begun to earn local respect at school. Her intimidating words were meant to make me cower in fear, but I was no longer afraid. She opened her mouth to speak, but before another word could escape, I threw her up against the neighbor's car on the walk home from school one day, and I beat her senseless. A large impenetrable stone grew around my heart that kept me from feeling remorse for my actions. The man watering his front yard seemed to be more concerned about us damaging his car than either of us. Mama disenrolled me the following day and sent me off to my third middle school in less than a year.

I often wondered if God had finally abandoned me. Nothing seemed to be working out for me, though I can't say that I put forth much effort to try. None of my father figures ever seemed to stick around long, so why would He, and my mother – well, she could only give to me what she possessed, and she always drew out of an empty well. In my heart, I knew that God loved everybody. Maybe, He just didn't like me.

Carnegie Middle School had a completely different atmosphere than Curtis Jr. High. The campus was brighter, and I made friends almost instantly. What I loved the most were the school assemblies. The Samoans would represent their culture by dressing up in their traditional hula skirts and war makeup. They would perform a dance and the female student body would scream as though we were all at an Usher concert. Looking at the oiled-down, vanilla-toned, bare chests of the fine Samoan boys would awaken my young flesh and its cravings. Yet, although I was surrounded by new friends and had a fresh start on a beautiful school campus, my heart was empty. Internally, I experienced the aching grief of loneliness.

By eighth grade, I was a professional ditcher. I had gotten really good at it until my teachers began to report my absences to Mama. Here I was again in the principal's office, but this time it was not for fighting. This time, I was being threatened with expulsion for excessive truancies. Little did they know, I had lost my place in the world and was being overcome by malignant shame. I wanted to run away from the trauma of the past, but I did not know where to go or who to trust with the filth of my heart. The next best thing was to avoid being near people who had the potential to see the real me, and since the classroom was filled with people, I avoided it altogether.

During our meeting with the principal, Mrs. Warner, she asked Mama, "Ms. Love, is this normal behavior for Zoe?"

Mama looked as though she wanted to be offended, and with a tight lip answered, "No, it's not."

"I don't mean to be intrusive, Ms. Love, but ever since Zoe joined us here at Carnegie, she has only attended the first week of class. Here we are on week four, and Zoe has been missing valuable class time. Her teachers are all very interested in getting to know Zoe but have not had the opportunity since she has been missing."

Mama looked annoyed as Mrs. Warner continued. "Is anything going on at home that we should know about? Maybe with that information, we can better help Zoe."

"Look, I appreciate your attention to detail, seeing that my daughter has missed three weeks' worth of class and you are just now noticing. What my daughter needs is not just a school that pays attention to the grades on her paper, but also the person she is within. Zoe is a remarkable girl; she just needs to be around people who can see that."

As I sat listening to their conversation, this one reality came to my mind: even though I'd felt lost, displaced, and unwanted for so long, the teachers had still noticed my absence. It helped me to realize that no matter how hard I tried, I was not invisible; someone saw me and felt the absence of my presence. The principal told my mother that

I would be serving detention every day after school to make up for the time I had missed during regular school hours. To my surprise and delight, I was given the task of assisting the agricultural teacher with tending to the school garden after hours. I didn't mind this sentence at all. In fact, I enjoyed the stillness of the garden and pruning the dead branches from the beautiful plants. There was no one there to look upon my wounds. The teacher was grateful to have help and seemed to enjoy my company. No one was there forcing me to have a conversation, so I didn't have to say a word unless I chose to; I chose to speak to the garden. Watching the water soak into the garden's dry soil as I watered it, brought hope that maybe, one day, someone would do the same for me. Didn't my mother see my thirst? Couldn't she see that I desperately thirsted for her time and attention? Did anyone notice that I was an unwatered, deserted garden, overridden with weeds and dead leaves, and in urgent need of sunlight?

Out of the desperate need to be noticed, I began to let visitors into the most sacred space within my garden. The people whom I had allowed to visit had only left behind their trash, polluting my garden. At 12 years of age, I let my next-door neighbor pluck my most fragrant rose from its place, my virginity, only to discard me among the weeds. I could have told him "No," but he begged and pleaded for it, and I had no defender to guard me, and teach me the value of my purity. My rose was gone, and so went a portion of my soul with it. Soon after, I welcomed other lovers to visit my garden, and I became a most gracious host. The numbness of my heart did not allow me to feel any shame as the boys in the neighborhood shared their stories of how they'd *had their way with me.* I became known as the neighborhood

"hood rat," but I didn't care. My body was my power, and sex was my new language. It was the one thing within my control and the only thing that took me away from the agony of abandonment. In exchange for a temporary lust for love, I let visitors pluck the flowers from the most intimate part of my garden, taking along with them the treasures of my soul.

CHAPTER 13

Reckless Abandonment

Those controlled by the flesh cannot please God.
Romans 8:8 (BSB)

"Zoe, ask your mom if we can smoke in your room." It wasn't hard to imagine the look on my face as my best friend Nicole offered such a ridiculous suggestion. We'd hit it off the first day we met at Banning High School and were more like sisters than friends. Although we were only in the ninth grade, we ran that campus.

"What? Niki, are you trying to get me killed?"

It never occurred to me that Mama knew I smoked weed. I'm sure there were times she noticed that some of her stash was missing, and other times when I came into the house reeking of its stench, but she never said anything that suggested she knew.

"Look. Would you rather go outside and walk around the block? Besides, it's hot out today! And you know if Michael and Mitchell see us, they're gonna be begging for a hit, and I don't feel like sharing," Nicole pouted, crossing her arms and making the face of a temperamental toddler.

Taking a deep breath, I thought about what Mama's reaction might be. My Mama was my homegirl. She was easy to talk to, and I could tell her anything. Usually, when I asked Mama for something, her first response would be, "No," but if I asked her enough times, she would eventually give in to my persistence, and say "Go ahead Zoe." I discovered early on that Mama did not like being hypocritical. She never liked to reprimand me for something that she struggled with in her own life. Mama let me make my own mistakes; she let me bump my own head and never criticized me for being a flawed human being. I only wish that she had been available to help me pick up the broken pieces of my soul along the way.

The sadness in Mama's eyes told the story of her wilted and shameful past. Her heart hurt for me. Mama's deepest and most heartfelt desire was to exemplify the character of a wise, loving mother, who could mentor, guide and lead me by example; yet the only way she knew how to cope with her life's regrets was to self-medicate with drugs, alcohol, and the attention of men. With each new year, I began to follow more and more in Mama's footsteps by pursuing her vices of drugs and men, with one exception: I took things a step further by joining a gang.

The street gang I joined was called "The Perverts," and my hood name was "Lil' Nympho." I didn't give myself that name; I didn't even know what it meant, although in all actuality, it was an accurate description of what I had become. I remember finding out that my big homie Tasha, who was only in the eleventh grade, had a one-year-old son. The discovery of a teenage girl in high school who already had a child made me change my mind about being a Pervert. She was my big homie, the one I looked up to, but in my heart, I wanted more for my life. When I told my crew that I was finished running with the Perv's, they did not let me go peacefully. The day I announced that I was making my exit, they followed me home from school calling out, "Bit*h, you ain't sh*t! We gonna beat your a*s." As soon as I got off the bus, I hit the corner at a brisk pace. There was no way that I would let them see me fearfully running, so as fast as I could, I zig-zagged my way through the streets that led toward home until they finally caught up to me. I knew what was coming, so I threw down my backpack and started throwing punches. I lost my footing when one of my now ex-homies punched me in the face and knocked me to the ground. This was now the second occasion that I'd gotten jumped, but this time, it was by a group of girls that I had once called "family." I went home with a busted lip, bruised ribs, and a mild concussion. Mama didn't even notice.

As I grew older, I could see that Mama blamed herself for my father's absence. She was now the mother of three girls, Chloe who was turning eight, Majesty who was only four, and I, Zoe, who was 14 going on 40. Each of us had different daddies. My father was only a shadow in her dark history, but the ghost of my father haunted Mama like the Ghost of Christmas Past. She seldomly mentioned his name, and Mama overcompensated for his absence by allowing me to come and go as I pleased with no consequence. Mama did all she could for us girls, but working long hours left little time, energy or attention for her to spare. Her comfort was her dysfunctional relationship with my youngest sister, Majesty's alcoholic father.

"Come on. I'll go with you," Niki said, her voice bringing me back to reality, and awakening me from my own thoughts. She grabbed my hand like an aggressive usher at a Baptist church.

"Ughhh!" was my only response. Trembling, I walked towards the kitchen and peeked inside. Mama was washing the dishes with her back towards us. I looked back over my shoulder to find Nicole grinning from ear to ear, looking as if she had already taken a few puffs of some good stuff. "Mama?" I said in a whisper. Mama turned her attention towards me. I stood petrified at the door as I tried to muster up the courage to speak the next words. "Is it okay if Niki and I smoke in my room?" My voice carried a tone of fear and innocence. Mama paused, so I continued. "We don't want to smoke outside in the open."

After a few seconds, Mama turned to look out of the kitchen window in front of her. After silently contemplating for several moments, she turned towards me again. "Okay," she replied somberly. Before she could change her mind, Niki and I hastily went to the room, lit a joint and filled the room with the aroma of weed as we puffed, puffed and passed.

Niki and I were two relentless ninth graders who loved running the streets with no adult supervision. Our high school days were filled with weed smoke, cute thugs and doing whatever felt good to us at the moment. Mama was too busy working and entertaining her own demons to notice that her firstborn was never home. I often stayed over at Niki's or with my boyfriend while he visited my garden. From time to time, I would go home just to check in on my little sisters, do a few chores and raid my mom's stash again. Then, I was back out in the streets.

Niki and I were notorious for being the flyest and the best dressed in the streets and at school. Oftentimes, we took her mom's car to the Crenshaw Mall and borrowed (without the intent of returning) clothes from Macy's, Nordstrom and JC Penney, which is how we stayed fly. At first glance at our attire, one would think we had very wealthy parents. However, if they peeked behind the scenes, they would only discover that our parents had very limited resources.

I learned just about everything from Niki. She taught me how to clean my house, do my hair, and stay savvy and street smart. The boys wanted us, while none of the girls liked us. At school, there were two girls, Katrina and Dee Dee, who despised us and kept threatening to fight us. Little did they know, Niki loved a challenge. I, on the other hand, was a lover, not a fighter. A peacemaker, not a warrior.

One day after school, they followed us onto our school bus. Niki whispered to me, "Zoe, after the next stop, I'm gonna turn around and punch Katrina in the face. You hop over the seat and get Dee Dee."

I was shocked and scared, but I could not let Niki know, so I replied, "Shouldn't we just wait until tomorrow?"

"No, Zoe! Can't you see that they got on our bus to follow us home? This ain't their bus! If we don't attack them first, they're gonna get off on our stop, and no one will be there to stop the fight."

Reluctantly, I agreed as the bus driver approached the next stop. My heart sank into the pit of my stomach as the door shut behind the students who exited.

"On the count of three," Niki said, as the bus started down the street again. "One..." I sat paralyzed as Niki continued and took off her shoes. "Two..."

I thought, *how do I dare say, "Wait, I'm not ready. I don't want to fight?"*

"Three!" Niki turned around and did just as she said she would. She punched Katrina right in the face, and all that could be heard was, "Ooooooooooh," from the kids on the bus.

I stayed seated and slowly turned to look back at Dee Dee, who didn't seem as eager to fight as Niki and Katrina. It went without saying that we were now obligated. So, I followed Niki's orders. I hopped over the seat and proceeded to punch Dee Dee in the head. However, she was much stronger than I was and managed to throw me onto the floor of the bus, face down. She climbed onto my back and began hitting me in the back of my head. I could hear the crowd's "Ooohs" and "Ahhhs" as I got my butt kicked.

Finally, the bus driver pulled the bus over and called for back-up on his radio. He started shouting at us to sit down and told us all that the police were on their way. As soon as we heard the word, "Police," everyone got quiet, and we scurried like mice back to our seats. Niki had worn a tube-top that day, which had been dislocated during the course of the fight. Now, every guy on the bus had a visual image of her bare breasts ingrained in their minds. Niki managed to pull her shirt up while she held her shoes in hand.

The bus driver ordered us off the bus. Niki and I were sitting in the back, so on our way off, we had to pass up Katrina and Dee Dee who were now sitting at the front of the bus. Niki went first and I followed slowly behind as we made our way towards the exit. I couldn't get off the bus like the loser I was without kicking Katrina on my way out, so, I did just that: I kicked Katrina's leg as hard as I could. She hopped up out of her seat, but before she had the chance to grab me, Niki took her shoe and hit her dead smack in the mouth with the heel, causing Katrina to fall backward into Dee Dee's arms, blood gushing from her mouth.

From that moment on, Niki and I were inseparable, so when the school principal expelled us both, sending us to different schools; my heart broke into a thousand pieces. I was transferred to Carson High School and Niki was sent to Narbonne High. We were not allowed to go to the same school, but that didn't stop us from seeing each other. After school, we would meet up, smoke weed and hang out with the neighborhood Crips. One by the name of Blue made me his girlfriend. He was the gangsta that all the Crips looked up to. Even though he was the head Nigga to be feared, to me, he was a fine gentle giant. I fell in love-lust with Blue and spent many a night climbing through his bedroom window and into his bed destroying my garden. I count it a miracle that I never became pregnant, though the lonely part of me wanted to be. Blue and I were always together, and when we weren't, we would find each other. Niki's boo was Lil' C. Together, the four of us were unstoppable.

One evening, Niki and I went to a house party, where we expected to have a good time with our boo's. I leaned up against the wall in the backyard checking out the scene, looking for my baby Blue. Niki made her home on the dance floor and was dancing like it was nobody's business. Suddenly, I heard a loud *POP, POP, POP.* Frightened screams followed as I watched people throw themselves over the backyard wall, placing a barrier between them and danger. Young teenagers took on the faces of scared little children calling for their mommies as they crouched down, longing for salvation. The Bloods who had shot up the party had done a drive-by and managed to hit one of their Crip rivals. A young teen boy, who was about 16 years old and had just joined the Crips, had been shot in the leg. He looked to be in shock as he waited for the ambulance to arrive. Niki and I didn't wait around for the police to come. We ran home to safety.

As I woke the next day to the sunlight piercing my eyes, I couldn't help but wonder about my future. With the lifestyle I was choosing, I felt the eerie presence of darkness chasing me down. I knew that if I did not begin to make some changes, one day, it would eventually catch up to me.

From the 10th to the 11th grade, Niki and I evolved from immature teenagers into young ladies, and the ache in my soul grew within me. I found myself spiraling out of control.

Niki and I welcomed a new friend named "Kami" to join us on our escapades. Kami was funny, outgoing and loved to club. Though her mother was present, she was fatherless, just like Niki and I. Kami had a way with the fellas, and when the three of us were together, our attire went from fly to sexy, and we *slayed all day*. I didn't think much about the impact I had on others until Blue and I were no longer an item. The careless, zombie-like nature that I had started to develop made me feel nothing the day that I slept with his cousin. It was only then that I learned that I had become a master of self-sabotage. In my heart of hearts, I cared for Blue, but the wickedness that began to flood my soul overshadowed the care that I felt for him. In his brokenness, he cussed me out in front of his crew. Even Niki was disgusted with me, although she remained a loyal friend. She was disappointed with me for breaking the heart of someone whom she had considered a big brother. Blue was livid and Niki was ashamed. As for me, I just went from lonely to lost, and from guy to guy – to girl.

"Hey, Z! What are you doing tonight?" Kami asked. She called my house one Friday evening, looking for something to do.

"Nothing. I'm bored. I'm just sitting on the couch eating Oreo cookies and watching BET. You want to come over?" I asked.

"I have something even better in mind. Let's go to a *party*!" Kami's enthusiasm was contagious, and it was easily transferred through the phone to me.

In an instant, I had an excitement of my own. I didn't ask where, when, or who would be at this party. I just said, "Okay! Let's go!"

Kami came and picked me up in her mother's Toyota. We hit the streets looking sexy in the moon light. I wore a hot pink, white-striped fitted two-piece outfit. The blouse exposed my twin girls in the front. They hung freely without the constraint of a bra and said, "Hello!" to every onlooker. The fitted skirt hung calf length, yet it attached itself to my thighs like Saran Wrap.

When we arrived at the party, we walked into the backyard where we heard 2Pac blasting from the DJ's speakers at a volume that was clearly loud enough to keep the neighbors awake. "All eyes on me," 2Pac sang, as if he knew we were coming. I looked around, scouring the crowd for a fella to lock eyes with. Only, there was not a single guy at this party. From the DJ to the dancers, not one guy!

"Kami, what type of party is this? There is nothing but females and Dikes here," I said, looking around the yard. As I turned towards Kami for a response, she was walking away holding the hand of a female who was dressed in oversized clothes. By the look in the girl's eyes, she obviously had a thing for Kami. Totally disappointed, I walked over to an unoccupied chair near the wall. As I took a seat, I felt the piercing stare of someone coming from my left. I looked over to see this chocolate figure coming towards me. I was confused as to whether it was male or female but could see that they wore their hair in two cornrows down the back. They had the broad chest and shoulders of a man, yet they were short in stature like a woman. As they came into the light, I saw that she was a female whose baggy clothing and demeanor gave her the resemblance of a male. In that moment, my curiosity for females awakened.

"Hey, how you doin'?" she asked. Her sensual voice sent a chill up my spine.

Not wanting to look interested, I frowned and did my best to look annoyed. "Look, I don't want to waste your time, so I'll let you know up front: I'm not into girls."

Unmoved by my statement, she replied, "Okay, I respect that. How about friends? Are you open to making a friend?"

DAMN! Stop talking so I don't change my mind, I thought to myself as I bit my bottom lip hard enough to make it bleed. "Umm, I guess I can be open to that." We sat and talked the whole night as Kami danced and drank herself into a stupor.

"Here, take my number." Beautifully handwritten on a napkin was her phone number. She slid it over to me. "I look forward to seeing you again, friend," she said, smiling at me.

Looking down at the napkin, it read "Penny." "Me too, Penny."

Niki, Kami and I were hustlers. We were introduced to a guy named Bo who seemed interested in our looks and promised us the opportunity to record our voices in a free studio recording session. In our opinion, each of us had nice singing voices, and had the potential to record our own album. Before long, we began envisioning ourselves as the next 702, an all-girl singing group that was popular at the time. Little did we know, Bo wore multiple hats. He was also a pimp.

"You girls interested in making some quick cash tonight?" Bo inquired.

"Always!" Niki didn't hesitate to answer, while I questioned in my mind what "making some extra cash" looked like.

"I have a job for you then. My boy is about to get married, and tonight is his bachelor party." Bo explained. "Well, I got a call saying that the strippers didn't show up."

Strippers? I thought. My heart sank. *I know this man is not about to ask us to go strip for a group of men.* The questions that immediately began to swirl around in my head needed answers, but I was too afraid to speak up for myself. There was also the issue of how I felt about my body, to begin with. My physique was not my greatest asset. My body had grown fully before its time, so my arms and breasts were covered in stretch marks, and this often made me self-conscious. The only time I didn't mind was when I was underneath somebody's sheets.

When we arrived at the groom's house, it looked like a home out of a magazine. Beautifully furnished with the intentional design style and eye for detail of a professional interior decorator. The men were waiting in the large living room with faces filled with hopeful expectation, waiting to have their fantasies realized. Niki and Kami hit the floor as soon as the music turned on. Removing their shirts and then their bras was no problem for them. Kami came ready with her thong, revealing her apple-shaped, dipped in dark chocolate bottom. The cash came flying at her. I, on the other hand, stood too scared to remove my clothes. The older gentleman that I danced for was unmoved; he could feel me trembling as I finessed my body across his. I'm sure that he could tell that inwardly, I was just a baby. I only took home a few dollars, while Kami and Niki walked away with hundreds. On the car ride home, I decided that this first-time stripping would also be my last.

My longing for a love that could satisfy only grew stronger and more intense as I filled my bed with lovers – lovers who would only contribute to the deteriorating patchwork of my broken soul. Joey, Tony, Nate, and even Penny all carried away with them pieces of my soul as they fondled my body and then fled my bed.

The only guy who did an even exchange was Eric. Eric became my sweetheart during the 11th grade. Eric loved to love me. I met Eric during summer school on our high school campus and thought he was a cutie pie. The tone of his voice made me melt as he spoke to me. Eric was a thug who was "down for whateva" and he wasn't scared of anybody. He would catch the bus with me and walk me home, right into 163rd Street and Central Avenue in Compton, California – his rival gang's territory. There wasn't a member of his hood there to watch his back. Eric was on the wrong side of the tracks; a gun could go off at any moment, and it would more than likely be aimed at him, yet Eric's desire for me was strong enough for him to risk his own life.

One day during class, Eric slipped me a note asking if I would spend the night with him. He said his mom would be out of town, and he wanted me to keep him company. "Okay," I replied on the little piece of paper. The next day, I brought my overnight bag to class, and he carried it for me the entire way to his apartment. Eric was gentle and thoughtful when it came to me. He loved holding my hand and treated me differently than the other guys. He cherished the time we spent together. On the way to his place, we stopped to get something to eat. When we finally arrived at the apartment, it was quiet. No one was home. I showered the events of the day off of my body and walked into the room where I met Eric. That night, two teenagers loved like adults until the sun rose on us. We drunkenly made our way to school the next day, as the night's events caught up with us. I slept in class and could hear Eric's boy asking for details.

The perfect gentleman responded, "Nigga, that's my lady, and I ain't sayin' sh*t."

Eric's infatuation towards me turned into an obsession. About four months after we began dating, Eric decided to surprise me with a tattoo of my name on his arm. He thought that it would cause me to stay around. However, I was a wanderer, and my roots never stayed in one place long enough for fruit to grow on my tree. What Eric didn't know was that I had Nate and Tony picking me up from school every other day. One day, I messed up and forgot that Tony was picking me up on the same day as Nate. I forgot that I had asked him to come get me in his ol' school Cadillac. I panicked when I realized that they were both standing outside of their cars, waiting for me. Instantly, I had to decide which one I was going to go home with.

As Niki and I approached them, with a look of bewilderment, I asked, "Niki, what should I do?"

Niki looked at me, rolled her eyes and just shook her head. Nate was about 27 and I was only 16, but he liked my hazel eyes and honey-brown skin. Niki had also cut my hair to match my sassy personality, which made me appear older than I really was.

"Nate, I got a call at school that my aunt died. I have to go home with my cousin today," I said as I watched Tony a few cars over, watching me. I'd made the lie up on the spot.

"Alright, baby girl. Call me later," Nate replied.

I took a deep breath as I walked over to Tony, who had a "Who is that Nigga?" look on his face, although he remained silent. Tony looked exotic with his long, silky, curly hair that he often kept in a ponytail. He was fine. I had a different relationship with Tony than I did with Nate. To Nate, I was a first prize trophy piece. We drove around in his Cadillac as he showered me with the finer things in life. However, when I was with Tony, we smoked weed, hung out together, and laughed all the time.

The day Nate and I almost became lovers is the day my life took a pivotal turn. I was now sixteen and my life was a cyclone of sex, lies and drugs, and unfortunately, my two little sisters, looked up to me. It wasn't long before they began to mimic my behavior.

One day after school, Nate picked me up with a fresh batch of chronic in his pocket. I invited him back to my house so we could smoke it in my bedroom. We lit a joint and the room became an oasis where the two of us got lost in each other. His masculine, father-like hands felt safe and secure as he touched my body. I leaned into him and smothered him with my chest. He began to massage the small of my back, and I straddled him, turning my face to the window. Just then, I saw two little faces peering inside. It was Chloe and Majesty, my now ten and six-year-old little sisters. My mouth flew open. I jumped off Nate and hurriedly shut the blinds.

"Get out of here!" I yelled. I sat in embarrassment, feeling ashamed for what my little sisters might have seen. I asked Nate to leave and then ran after my sisters, scolding them, and telling them to *not* do the same.

Shortly after the incident, Mamma called me into her room as I prepared to go out for the evening. "Zoe, from now on, when you go on a date, you have to take Chloe with you." Mamma demanded.

"What? But I –" I began. Then, after realizing that I was about to give my secrets away, I shut my mouth. Mama did not know that I would get high on different guys in the same night. She was not around to see her baby girl high on ecstasy and drinking alcohol. Mama didn't know that the lack of fulfillment in her soul was the same one that now contaminated mine.

My little sisters loved me and wanted to be just like me, but there was no way that I could allow that to happen. Chloe followed me around like a shadow when I was home. She was the most beautiful and bright-eyed little girl I had ever seen. I envied how smart she was; she was a straight-A student and had a personality that was as cute as can be. Majesty was a naughty little girl, but she could get away with murder because she had a smile so bright, you could not help but love her. Chloe and Majesty both had fathers who cared for and admired them. I couldn't understand why my father didn't do the same. What was so wrong with me that made him not choose me?

The painful discovery of my father's other family desecrated the little remains of my wounded heart. To make matters worse, the children that he nurtured, loved, and protected were siblings that I'd wished for. Here I was, sixteen and he had a son who was the same age as I. This news only served as proof that something was indeed wrong with me. He also had four older daughters which meant that I have older sisters, which was something that I had always dreamed of having – sisters who could teach me what to do, and what NOT to do. I so desperately needed a guide, someone to steer me around the pitfalls that I had ignorantly wandered into throughout my life.

Seeing the eyes of my two little sisters peer through the blinds of my bedroom window, I knew at that moment that I had to be for Chloe and Majesty what I felt I had needed the most; someone whom they could look up to – a big sister. I knew that if I did not make a drastic change for the better, my choices would lead me down the pathway to death; and to death, they would follow.

CHAPTER 14

The Purest Love

"I have found the one whom my soul loves."

Song of Solomon 3:4 (JUB)

Everything and everyone I touched seemed to wither like the autumn leaf. *I can't continue like this*, I constantly thought. Although my demeanor was sassy, sexy and stoic on the outside, the little girl who lived within me cried daily, *somebody… anybody... please save me!*

I abandoned little Zoe. I had left my younger self alone in a dark closet, and I shut the door on her, locking her inside. Within myself, I cried continuously in agony, longing for someone to come and rescue me from - me. When I closed my eyes, I could see a mental image of my younger self, sitting in a fetal position, curled up into a ball in the corner of the closet, rocking back and forth, covered in my own feces. Being in this position for so long, caused the fecal matter to harden like rocks of clay on the skin of my tiny frail and weak body. My hair, matted in knots, and filled with a filthy residue because of the years of neglect. Who would dare want to touch me, when I could not stand my own sight?

Young Zoe no longer recognized what pure love was. It had become a tainted memory beyond her grasp, only to eventually become forgotten. By the time I reached the little girl in the closet, she had been there for years. Her heart had grown cold like the coldest of winters, and little Zoe had become feral and unrecognizable. The elder version of myself was content with leaving little Zoe behind locked doors. As long as I kept her there, I didn't have to look at how filthy she was. I was not reminded of her guilt and shame, and the trauma that produced her pain, or the abuse of her molester. I didn't have to live with the reality that she grew up sexually active before she was even a teen, or the pain she inflicted on herself. I could lock her away and ignore the lies that said, she was not worthy of knowing the pure love that little girls receive from their fathers. Locking little Zoe away left her with ruminating thoughts that told her she was un-worthy, she was an embarrassment, and that she wasn't worthy of pursuing. One day, I finally cracked the door open and peeked inside.

My Lula and I were spending girl time together one weekend. Now that I was older, we hung out like the best of friends - friends who loved good food and good conversation. Uncle Troy had gone out of town, leaving his dogs unattended, and had asked Lula to check in on them from time to time and feed them. Lula brought me along with her, and off we went to Uncle Troy's place. When we arrived, I remember looking around the condominium thinking, *this is where I need to be*. Apparently, my thoughts spoke aloud, because Lula responded as though she had been eavesdropping.

"Why don't you ask Uncle Troy if you could come stay with him again?" Lula suggested. I hadn't lived with Uncle Troy since the 6th grade. It was the beginning of summer and in just a few months, I would officially be a senior. I looked at my Lula and admired her courage to change directions in the middle of life's course.

"I want to, Lula, but I can't leave Mama. She's been making comments recently about how having me has saved her life. Lately, she has been saying that she needs me home to help her with Chloe and Majesty. What's going to happen if I leave her now?"

"Don't you worry your pretty little head about that, Zoe Maree," my Lula said in her calm and assuring voice. "Just ask her and don't delay."

The phone rang with a gentle buzz as I sat nervously on the other end rehearsing what I would say when Uncle Troy answered. The heart-to-heart that I'd had with Mama had gone better than expected. I nervously asked her if I could go live with Uncle Troy for my senior year of high school, and to my surprise, she had enthusiastically agreed to let me go. Now, all I had to do was ask Uncle Troy.

"Hello."

"Hi Uncle Troy. This is Zoe."

"I know who this is! How is my Zoe?" he asked.

"I'm doing pretty good. I... I wanted to ask you how you felt about me coming to live with you while I finished my last year in high school?" My own forwardness shocked me. *Maybe I should have engaged in more conversation before I asked,* I thought to myself.

"Of course, you can!" I thought my ears were deceiving me as Uncle Troy continued. "And I already know what school you will attend. John Muir High School is where your cousin Megan goes. It will be good for you girls to look after each other and keep one another company. I will make a few phone calls as soon as we get off the phone," he said.

All at once, my heart, which had been beaten down by abandonment, rejection, hurt, and shame, became filled with the warmth of acceptance. I felt hopeful for the first time in my life. My eyes watered as I held back the tears. This was not like the other times that I had gone from school to school as a lonely, wandering soul; this was of my choosing. This time I wasn't being passed along; no, not this time. Now, I was determined to chose my life's course. This time I chose to live. This would be the death of my past and every choice that led me down Death Valley. It was the death of the insecure Zoe, and the resurrection of the fully-known and fully-loved Zoe Maree. This was *my* new beginning.

The end of summer had drawn near. I made it a point to pack my most valuable things, leaving behind the things that reminded me of my wilted past. My room at Uncle Troy's condo was fully furnished, so I wouldn't need much. Simple, yet elegant is how I would describe it, and smelled of lavender. The antique vanity, mirror, couch and unique art framed on the walls made me feel like I was maturing. I was finally at home. I walked around the room slowly taking in this new beginning. I looked out of the big beautiful arched window that consumed the wall in my room and thought, *Maybe God does like me after all.*

Life at John Muir High School was a vastly different world from the one I had left behind. At first glance, the school appeared much different than the other two high schools that I had previously attended. The campus was clean and surrounded by glorious live oak trees. The view of the beautiful San Gabriel Mountains in the near distance made me feel calm and at peace.

To my delight, the students at this school were interestingly different, and not at all like the kids back home. Here, they weren't getting lit in the bathrooms. Students actually went to class and were at school to learn. They were full of purpose and vision. Conversations were not about who had a baby, where to buy the best weed, or how ol' girl was giving it up in the boys locker room. Here, there was talk about how many colleges you applied to and betting on which one was going to send you the first acceptance letter. All of this talk made me begin to care about my grades. I went from being the student who ditched class on a regular basis, to being the girl making A's and B's. It helped that Uncle Troy didn't accept anything less. High school, once the place I'd dreaded, had now become the place I loved to be.

John Muir was also the place where I met my first love. Prior to meeting Christian Anthony, I had considered Blue to be the love of my life. However, my feelings for Blue did not even come close to how Christian made me feel. He was everything I *thought* I needed. Though my environment changed, my heart still longed to have intimacy – the type of intimacy that would allow another to look deeply in – to – me.

One sunny cool day, I came dressed to impress, as always. Although I couldn't bring my bestie Niki with me to John Muir, everything she taught me about fashion and the knowledge of how to slay, I had preserved. I rocked six-inch heels on campus daily, and Uncle Troy made sure that I looked not only fly but classy, which was a major upgrade from the overtly provocative outfits that I had previously worn. Video chicks had nothing on me! I maintained my short haircut and went to a local hairstylist. She was known to divinely replicate any hairstyle from a photograph. I was the new student at the school, but more than that, I was the new senior, which made me mysterious. Although I was straight outta Compton, my sass and sex appeal made me the fantasy of every player on the football team.

Big Chris was a big teddy bear. He was shy, tender and quiet. The way he got my attention sums him up very well: he asked Corey, a friend of his, to convince me to take his number, which he had written on a piece of paper torn off of a lunch bag.

"Hey, what's your name?"

I looked over my shoulder to see if the handsome shorty was talking to me. I realized I was the only one around and replied, "Zoe, but you can call me Z."

"What up, Z? My name is Corey. My boy wanted me to give you his number," he said, pointing in the direction of a group of guys. I couldn't tell which of his boys he was referring to. "If you decide to call, it's all good. If not, no hard feelings."

"Why didn't he bring me his number himself?" I asked as I looked down at the wrinkled paper.

"Don't tell him that I said this, but... he's shy."

I giggled. "What? Can't a grown man be shy?" Corey questioned with a smirk. "I guess?" is all I replied. There was something about hearing those words that made the nurturer in me arise. *He's shy?* I thought to myself as I slipped the piece of paper into my back pocket. I watched Corey walk away with a sense of accomplishment.

Big Chris. Just the thought of him made my soul churn and tears well up in my eyes. He was the possessor of my heart and the love of my soul. Just one glance at his silky, milk chocolate skin, almond-shaped eyes, and muscular build, which made him about nine inches taller than I was, even when I was in my heels, made me want to scream for Mama! Christian was my heartbeat. Unfortunately, I was too naive to know just how much of a ladies' man Big Chris was.

Late one evening, while out with my girl Ashley, we drove the long route to my cousin Megan's house. Although it was dark outside and hard to see, I managed to catch a glimpse of a couple, as the two shadowy figures leaned against the trunk of a car. I asked, "Ashley, did that look like Big Chris?" She was too busy driving to tell, and I dared not ask her to turn the car around. My heart didn't want to believe that it could be him, especially since he was due for an evening with me in less than an hour.

Megan lived on a quiet street in the hills of Altadena, where one could hear the howls of coyotes, and occasionally, the trotting of a deer's hooves. Big Chris arrived at Megan's house on time. My man was here.

"Did I just see you on Altadena drive?" I questioned him.

"Me? Nawww. I was at home before I came here."

Love-lust blinded my eyes and made me ignorant to the truth when it came to Big Chris. He and I had become intoxicated with each other. We smoked weed together after school, and I spent late nights over at his house breaking in his new mattress. He was not shy about telling all of his boys how he had me on my back most nights or about sharing the intimate details of our passion. One of his boys, Melvin, didn't like the way Chris exploited my name, and one afternoon on campus, he told me. Melvin felt sorry for me. He might have even seen the beauty beyond my physique. Later on, Melvin would ask me to the senior prom. I said "Yes," only to later cancel in hopes that Big Chris would come to his senses and ask me. He never did. So was the nature of our impure relationship. Lust, sex, lies - repeat.

Here I was out hitting the streets again, but this time it was with my best friend, Ashley, whom I had known since the first time I had come to live with Uncle Troy. Ashley and I went all the way back to the third grade. She was a sweetheart with a well-timed sense of humor, and though many years had passed between the third and twelfth grade, she had always seemed to find a way to get in touch with me. She was what many like to call a P.Y.T (pretty-young thang). Ashley was tall with a caramel skin tone, and jet-black hair that reached past her shoulders. My cousin Megan and Ashley were my new ride-or-die friends throughout my senior year. I marveled at the pride Ashley's mom and dad took in their daughter's achievements. Ashley was the only friend I ever knew who had the presence of both her mom and dad in her life. On her 16th birthday, they surprised her with a brand-new BMW. We were bad-ass 16-year-olds in a smoke gray BMW that was fresh off the lot, cruising down Sunset Boulevard in Los Angeles, bumping to Lil' Kim songs that are too vulgar to mention. We were trusted enough by our parents to come and go as we pleased. Though life seemed exciting and fun, it felt void of purpose and meaning.

Megan was not only my cousin; she was my friend. Like Ashley, Megan also had her mom and dad present to raise and protect her. Ashley and Megan's parents were some of the only examples that I had ever seen of married couples. Uncle Troy was not married, Mama was not married, and Lula and Grampa were no longer married. Not many in my immediate family were.

At school, I respected the friendships that Megan had with her track buddies, and she welcomed me into her inner circle of friends without hesitation. Megan and Ashley were good girls – virgins, unlike me. Then again, all of my friends were.

"Zoe, there is a youth service happening tonight at my church. Come with me."

I didn't know if Megan was asking me a question or if she was making a statement. "Uhhh... okay," I promised. That was one of many promises that I left unfulfilled with Megan. Each time she would ask, my response was the same.

"Okay. I'll go." Another promise broken.

I did not grow up in church. In fact, I wasn't even sure I understood the concept of church. Mama and I had only attended service on special occasions – Easter and Christmas. Mama had always taught us girls that God was real and to be revered, to always say our prayers, and to treat others the way we wanted to be treated. But church? The few rare experiences that I'd had in church were not memorable enough for me to want to voluntarily attend again.

I can't seem to recall, even to this day, how we ended up in the parking lot of Victory Bible Full Gospel Baptist Church. We pulled up in Megan's ol' school champagne-colored BMW.

I looked out of the passenger window and saw Big Chris entering the building.

"What is Christian doing here?" I asked Megan.

"Where are we?" Megan opened her door and shut it closed behind her, as if to say, *Let's go!* Stepping out of the car, I had no idea that this evening would become one of the most memorable, indelible, inerasable, indescribable moments *of my life*. The trajectory of my existence was about to change, and I had no inclination of what was to come.

Megan led me into the building. The ambience in the room did not feel like the other churches that I previously attended. The atmosphere was tranquil and calm. I looked around at the plush setting. There were green chairs, green carpet, and people seated facing a large stage that had three stairs leading up to a transparent podium. Megan led me to my seat as she spoke and said "Hello" to the people who had already arrived. She took her seat, and I sat down next to her. I sat waiting for an explanation about what was about to happen or what I should be doing, but it never came.

Soon after, a woman got up and took her place behind the podium. She began to welcome us all to an evening of Bible study and announced that shortly, we would break out into smaller groups according to our age range. One by one, she called out certain group names, and individuals started to rise from their seats and head toward their designated group's area. Megan arose and glanced at me, as to beckon me to follow her, so I did. We exited the sanctuary and walked to a separate dimly-lit building. The walls of the entire room were covered with banners that read, "Youth Radical for Christ" in big bold golden letters.

As we took our seats, I felt a warmth in the room. It wasn't a warmth from the room's temperature but from a loving presence that filled the air. A beautiful petite woman stood at the front of the room. She introduced herself as Pastor Liza Dion and invited us in. We were an intimate group of no more than ten people, and Big Chris was among us. Once everyone took their seats, she opened the evening with a word of prayer. After praying from the depth of her soul, the tiny lady opened her mouth and discussed the topic of the evening's Bible study. She began by saying, "Tonight, we are going to experience the power of surrender."

Immediately, her words open a portal to my soul that made me feel, exposed and vulnerable as she unknowingly shined a spotlight on the issues of my life that I thought were hidden. With every word she spoke, I sat paralyzed and unable to move, for I was held captive by the fear of being seen. For years, I had tried to hide the part of myself that lived beneath my own skin, the part that I did not allow others to see, and the place in me that was often concealed by guilt and shame.

During her short sermon, Pastor Liza unknowingly told everyone who I was without my permission. She unlocked the door to my soul and let everyone see the lost, lonely, and abandoned little girl living on the inside of me. She boldly told everyone that I was rejected by my biological father and sought solace in the arms of any lover who would have me. She revealed the inner part of my insecurity and my need to people please so that others would love and accept me. Or, *at least*, that is what I heard her say.

Pastor Liza spoke to the devastation of my pain and preached the truth to every lie that I had believed. She reminded us that God is not like man; He doesn't throw us away, and there is no wound that He is not willing to heal. Pastor Liza told us that God wants to become our Abba

Father and adopt us all as His sons and daughters. *What does it mean to be a daughter to the only living God?* I wondered.

As she brought her words to a close, she paused while peering intensely into each of our wounded hearts. She stepped from behind the podium that hid her petite figure, grabbed a chair and turned it to face her audience. Taking a seat, she sat up straight and spoke intently, as though she wanted to ensure that we did not miss a single word.

"There is a God who will never - and I mean never - leave nor will He fail you. God promises us in Psalm 23 that even when you walk through the darkest valley of your life with the shadow of death pursuing you, you don't have to be afraid, because He is right there with you. He is your greatest defender, your champion." She paused and smiled before continuing.

"He knew every challenge you would ever face, and yet, he has not allowed it to destroy you, because He is an intentional God, and He has a plan for you that supersedes your ability to imagine."

"It's time for you to comprehend who you are. In Christ, you are royalty, and no matter what mistakes you have made in the past, or even today, as sons and daughters, you can run to Him and not from Him. We all have a choice - choose to run to Him. In Genesis chapter 3, Adam and Even hid themselves in the garden. Can you imagine hiding from the one who created you, formed you from the dust of the ground then breathed His very breath into your lungs, only to hide? Why do you think they did that?" Pastor Liza paused and awaited a response.

A brave soul slowly raised their hand. "Yes, James."

James hesitantly replied, "Were they afraid?"

"Yes" she answered and said, "Fear caused them to forget their creator. I would also add, they hid because of their shame. Shame causes you and I to hide our faces from God instead of running into the arm of our creator - the one who saves our souls."

"His word says, "Then the man and his wife heard the sound of the LORD God as he was walking in the garden in the cool of the day, and they hid from the LORD God among the trees of the garden. But the LORD God called to the man, "Where are you?" He answered, "I heard you in the garden, and I was afraid because I was naked; so I hid.""

"Instead of running to God, Adam and Eve hid themselves in the garden, because of the shame their sin produced. Could you imagine what God's response might have been if Adam would have simply said "God, here I am. I'm sorry. I made a mistake. I have sinned and disobeyed your command to not eat of the forbidden tree. Please forgive me!" Rather, Adam gave God an excuse. "It was the woman you gave me. She gave me the fruit and I ate it." Adam blamed Eve, and made excuses instead of humbling himself in surrender. When we surrender, we resist the urge to blame or justify ourselves. So, what does it mean to Surrender? Surrender is the ability to lay down your plans and seek the Lord and His will with all of your heart. Surrender to Him today. Lay it all down – the pain of your disappointments. Come lay it down."

"His word says that He is patient, slow to become angry and willing to wait for you. He is waiting for you to come to Him and surrender your grief, shame, confusion and depression. Surrender the guilt of your sin.

Sometimes, we choose to hold on to things that are draining the life out of us, because it is all we know. The pain becomes so familiar to us that we forget what it's like to live without it. We find ways to cope by giving our bodies away to feel loved, because the pain of abandonment and rejection, others self-mutilate to numb themselves. Let Him show you that He can take all of your broken pieces and put you back together better than you were before, and He can do it this very day. You don't have to leave carrying the weight of your sin. You don't have to leave here today, the same way you came."

Pastor Liza stood up and gave an invitation for us to come up and receive individual prayer. Without thinking, my body and soul conspired against me, as I took my first step towards her. Everyone in the room seemed to disappear; they faded away with each step I took. Then, there was just Pastor Liza and I. She was even more lovely up close. Her voice carried the tone of a loving mother, yet her hands seemed to carry the power of 10,000 men. Though her physique was small, the woman standing on the inside of her was a spiritual giant.

As I stood before her in the presence of my newly-found loving Savior, she lifted my hands. Then, she placed her hands on my chest.

"He has loved you before you were a thought within your mothers imagination, and today, you get to love Him back." She said. Her words encompassed me, swaddling me like a warm blanket.

I poured my love upon Him with my tears. I closed my eyes as I gave into the overwhelming presence of God that was in the room. In that moment, I wailed for the little girl inside of me – the little girl that I had abandoned for so long. Pastor Liza had given little Zoe the permission that she needed to finally come out of the dark. With my eyes still closed, I saw myself enter into the closet where little Zoe lay, curled up into a ball. "You can come out now" I spoke gently to little Zoe. "It's time for you to live, Zoe." I spoke to her every fear, and embraced her. I told the younger me that Christ had come to set us free. We we're now safe, and it was time to come out from our hiding place.

I opened my eyes at the sound of Pastor Liza's voice. She spoke in a whisper and recited the scriptures in my ear.

"Jesus died so that you can live. It's time for you to live and His blood is able to cleanse you of all unrighteousness. Though your sins be as scarlet, they shall be as white as snow; though they be red like crimson, they shall be as wool." I felt the word of God washing me as she quoted Isaiah 1:18, and 1 John 1:7.

I stood there, now fully enveloped in this woman's arms, weeping with tears of lament, asking God to come into my life and cleanse me. All the pain that I had refused to allow myself to feel *for years* came rushing to the surface of my heart. The shame and guilt lifted with each tear that fell from my eyes as I surrendered.

Pastor Liza held me in her arms for what felt like hours. Upon the final tear, she cupped my face in her hands, looked me in my eyes and asked, "What is your name?"

"Zoe," I replied though breathless.

Her eyes lit up as she continued, "Do you know what your name means?"

"Yes, it means life," I replied.

Pastor Liza stared at me as though waiting to hear more. "Zoe, your name means 'Abundant Life!' In this life, you will discover that your purpose is being birthed out of your pain. Abba wants to use your pain to reveal to you the prevailing power of His love. This grace is not for you only, but as you journey through your own healing, you will become a midwife for others, and they too, will be rescued from the power of darkness. Then, they will become born again believers who step into their true identity in Christ, and you will witness God birth His masterful purpose in their lives."

The ice that encased my heart melted, and in that moment, I came alive. I could hear God's voice through her words. I knew for the first time the tranquility and purity of GOD'S LOVE, and I finally knew it in the absence of lust.

CHAPTER 15

In Full Bloom

"Forget the former things; do not dwell on the past.
See, I am doing a new thing!"
Isaiah 43:18-19 (NIV)

"And I am convinced that nothing can ever separate us from God's love. Neither death nor life, neither angels nor demons, neither our fears for today nor our worries about tomorrow—not even the powers of hell can separate us from God's love. No power in the sky above or in the earth below—indeed, nothing in all creation will ever be able to separate us from the love of God that is revealed in Christ Jesus our Lord." – Romans 8:38-39 (NLT)

I closed my Bible as I sat on the black leather sofa in my bedroom. It was early morning, and the sun peeked through my blinds as to say, *Good Morning!* Uncle Troy stood at my bedroom door, waving, "Have a great day," he said, right before heading to work. A few months had passed since I met the one whom my soul loves, and all I could think about was Jesus. There was this new swelling of my emotions, only it was not birthed out of pain as before. My heart was fully overwhelmed by this new discovery of who God is - and His love for me. I loved to be near Him in the morning. That was our time of intimacy. He satisfied my innermost longings like no other lover ever could. Inhaling deeply, I pondered the depth of the words I'd just read. Looking around my room, I reflected on the moment we first met. I felt refreshed, yet I could not escape the tears. *Cleansing* tears. I cried until my tears watered the garden of my soul. That same garden that I had once allowed men to trample and thieves to break in and plant weeds. That garden where boys and men had plucked my flowers and weed smoke polluted the air.

Now, my garden was finally beginning to bloom. Flowers were budding, butterflies danced, plants were flourishing, and birds - they were singing beautiful melodies. The cool breeze blew pollen through the air, and the sweet aroma was how I imagined the breath of God to be. My garden, once full of decay and debris, was now the place where the little girl inside of me could roam safely and freely and embrace her newly found destiny. Little Zoe was finally healing.

In the solace of my bedroom, I shut my eyes and envisioned myself sitting in the center of a fully bloomed garden with little Zoe. After being bathed in the garden's stream, she was now clean and smelled of white roses. Beautifully clothed in a regal purple and royal blue gown that shimmered in the light of the sun, little Zoe sat straight up while leaning back onto my chest, taking in the beauty of the garden. I imagined myself running my fingers through her hair and her fragrance rising up into my nostrils. I inhaled her essence. Our heartbeats were synchronized, our breaths flowed in rhythm – little Zoe and I were one. As we both sat listening to the melodies of the birds' songs and taking in the glory of God, she turned, faced me and looked up at me. Her eyes, the color of an autumn sky, were smiling, and they shone with the brightness of the sun.

"Hi there!" I said to the little me.

Without a word, little Zoe took my hands and held them. The warmth of her tiny hands felt comforting, as though they possessed great healing.

In a gentle whisper, she said, "I forgive you."

Her words caught me off guard. I didn't know how to respond. I just closed my eyes, buried my face in my hands, and cried, my tears washing my soul – again. When I finally opened my eyes, I was in my bedroom, yet the fragrance of little Zoe still lingered.

The hunger in my soul for God's word beckoned me to a place of intimacy with Him. I found myself fully indulging in the word of God in search of all the verses about love. Although Romans 8:38 had become my favorite Bible scripture, I was still trying to fully comprehend its meaning. The more time I spent with God, the more He revealed the purity of His love for me, and I began to understand that what Big Chris and I had identified as love, was really a fleshly desire to satisfy the cravings of our wounded souls. Yet, I couldn't control the reality that I still yearned for him. After a few minutes of pondering, while seated on the couch in my room, I pulled out my laptop and began to type UrbanDictionary.com into the web browser. I felt the need to search for a term that I had never heard of before. When the dictionary popped up, I typed the word "lovelust" into the search bar and pressed enter. The results revealed the definition:

> *Lovelust: An extremely strong and powerful feeling, yearning, craving, and desire to be with someone, know more about them, have them in your life. That new and wonderful in-love-like feeling that reaches deep down inside and outside your body, that you can't get out of your mind, your body, your heart, and your soul.*

It became very clear to me that what I'd shared with Christian was lovelust, yet I knew the place within my heart that Chris occupied, only had room for one. I wanted now more than ever for Jesus Christ to fill that space. It was time for me to let Chris go.

One evening while soaking in the bathtub, I laid in the water silently praying to God, asking Him to give me the strength to do what would honor Him the most.

"God, You know how I feel about Chris, and how I desire to love him. You were there when I inwardly vowed to never break up with him. I have made him my everything, and I do not want to let him go. But, if this is not the man that You have for me, I surrender our relationship to You, and I will release him. It will be one of the hardest things I have ever had to do, Lord. It's gonna break my heart, but I know that what You have for me is greater than any pain that I may feel for a moment, and You are the healer of my heart."

There was no need for God to come and trouble the water, I knew what I needed to do. Still lying in the water, I picked up the phone and dialed Chris's number.

"Hello," his melodic voice answered.

If I didn't get right to the point, I knew that I would change my mind, so I said,

"Chris, I think it's best if we take a break for a while."

"Okay, cool!" was his eager reply.

Okay? I thought. *How dare you agree, especially so quickly with no questions about why or anything!* My emotions wanted to scream, but I knew that God had just opened the door for me to go through, leaving Chris behind. God himself had answered my prayer.

In surrendering to God, I had to let Chris go. Although I had been consumed with thinking of him every second of every hour of the day, this experience helped me to realize that Chris did not feel the same way about me. I had idolized Chris and placed him on the throne of my heart – a place that only One God could reside. All of my life, I had wanted – needed – someone to love me in a way that would fill the gaping hole inside of me, but the whole time, God had been trying to reveal to me that only He could satisfy my soul.

Megan did not have to beg me to go to church with her anymore. My addictions to men and external things began to subside as my soul craved more and more of the presence of God.

Six months had gone by, three since my final conversation with Chris. On one Sunday morning, I sat in the sanctuary listening to the pastor preach healing to our souls. In the corner of my eye, I saw Chris walk in with a girl, hand in hand. Though I expected to feel the sting of seeing Chris with someone else, my hunger for God to fill every part of my being cried louder than my hunger for Chris.

The message that morning came like a consuming fire, straight down from Heaven. The pastor read from the book of Ezekiel chapter thirty-seven and preached to all of our dry bones. He read the words of Ezekiel aloud and prophesied the rebirth of us all.

"God will cause His breath to enter into your dry bones and you will come to life!" He spoke with a loud voice. "Then you will know that the Lord has spoken."

The pastor cut right to the point during the message, yet he took his time while giving the altar call.

"God wants to restore your mind, body, heart and soul. Let Him breathe *new* life into your spirit today. Your dry bones *can* live again. There is a new life awaiting you."

He held out his hand as to extend an invitation to each thirsty soul.

"How can this be, Lord?" I questioned silently.

"How is it that You can take all of my sin, my filth and my shame and give me a new life?"

"Come and drink from the well that will never run dry," were the final closing words of the pastor, and without hesitation, I went. Like lost sheep, many drew near to receive prayer. Pastor Jon, the youth pastor was available, so I made my way to him. PJ was a tall and slender man whose eyes seemed to penetrate parts of me that I did not want anyone to see, yet there was a tenderness about him that made him appear trustworthy. He rested his hand gently on my forehead and began to pray for me. His words began in a hushed tone, but the intensity of his prayer grew with his sincerity. Each word pierced and forced its way into my heart. With fervor, Pastor Jon began to thunderously declare,

"You have a bright future! Girl, your future is bright!"

The presence of God was so overwhelming that I screamed,

"I can't take it; I can't take it!"

I began to pull away from his hand as I fell to the floor, weeping. I knew that God had forgiven me, but I had not yet known how to receive His forgiveness. *How could I be worthy of a bright future?* I wondered as I wept. *Would Pastor Jon have spoken those words to me if he had known where I had been? Would he even want to pray for me if he had known that I'd lost my virginity at the fragile age of 12 and all that I had done since?* I questioned.

"God, how can my future be bright when my past is so dark?" I wailed.

With puffy eyes, I reached for a tissue to dry them. In a slow crawl, I made my way to the nearest chair I could find.

Then, in an attempt to hide, I kneeled down on the ground and wept with my head buried in the seat of the chair. As I sobbed, the feeling of being watched swept over me, though not from a far distance, but from nearby. At once, the empty chair was filled with the presence of God in whose lap I now cried. He comforted me as a parent comforts a child, and without uttering a word, His words entered deep into my being, letting me know that He will never let me go. His gentle whisper reminded me that He alone was my Abba. My purpose, though birthed out of my pain, was a necessary part of my journey. He let me know that His word is true, and none of my suffering would be wasted, but it would be used to comfort the broken. I could feel the love of a Holy father, the one I had been searching for all along. His words spoke of a commitment to never leave me, and a promise to be with me continually. God's healing words soothed the ache in my soul, and in this moment, I was hopeful. I felt new. I was free. Free to receive His salvation. Free to forgive and be forgiven. Free to be healed of the trauma from the past and made whole. Free to come alive in the presence of the Lord. Free to be all that God had intended for me to be before my very existence. Free to love out of a pure heart.

Daily, I began listening for the sound of His voice. After all this time, God was the "more" that I had been searching for. Now, He was right here to let me know that He had been with me all along. He was with me in my despair, and He had become my savior. My life was just beginning, and my journey was nowhere near complete. My church would become my home, and the people, my family.

During one of our youth nights, Pastor Jon mentioned a special purification service. We were offered the opportunity to recommit our bodies, hearts, minds and souls to Christ. Many of us had not kept our virginity, although others had. However, whether we were virgins or not, this service was our chance to make our vows to Jesus. For those of us who had not waited, it would be a time of recommitment, and for those who had waited, it would be a commitment to wait until marriage before giving their bodies to someone else. After he explained what it was, I immediately wanted desperately to be a part of it.

I was so ashamed of the thought that I did not know the number of men I had slept with; I'd lost count many years before. I knew in my heart that this service was specifically designed for me. I was filthy and needed a clean slate. After our many sessions discussing what it meant to have a pure heart and to preserve our bodies for marriage, I was ready. Internally, I had been made new, but I wanted the physical part of me to be made new, too. I knew what it was like to give a piece of my soul away to a man. The emptiness that came after lying in someone's bed was all too familiar to me, and that agony - I wanted nothing to do with anymore.

The day finally came for us to publicly make our vows before the Lord. The church was decorated as if for a wedding, and there was a beautiful banner hanging in the sanctuary that said *Worth the Wait* in large, bold print. Many of my new friends had invited their parents to the service. Megan's mom, dad, sister and nephew had come to support her big decision to wait. I looked around in the crowd trying to find a familiar face that belonged to me, but to no avail. A part of me was sad, and then I remembered the Lord whispering to me, "I am with you – always."

On that day, I walked up to the pastor, placed my hand in his, and repeated my vows to the Lord after him:

"God, I promise to Honor you within my body. My body is not my own, I am the temple of your holy dwelling and I will honor you in my body."

"Abba, I promise to abstain from the lustful desires of my flesh. Give me the grace I will need to do so, and I will keep myself pure for the husband that you are repairing for me."

"Jesus, I promise to love you through my obedience to your word, and to set my heart's affections on the eternal things above, and not on the temporal things of this world."

I knew that my commitment would come with its challenges, and my vows would be tested, yet I was willing to do whatever it took to draw nearer to God. In reality, I had no idea what temptations lie ahead, and that I would succumb.

He placed a ring on my index finger with the letters "WTW" on it that stood for *Worth the Wait*. I knew that my commitment would come with its challenges, but I was willing to do whatever it took to draw nearer to God.

I looked out into the crowd and saw Christian sitting in the corner staring at me, my heart did not flutter, and my emotions stood still. At that moment I knew that the place in my heart that he captured, had been released. He no longer conquered my heart. I suppose he knew that he was not willing to trade temporal physical pleasure for intimacy with the Heavenly Father, so he did not participate. In my heart, God was worth it, and now, so was I.

From that day forward, I experienced the joy and peace of the Lord in ways I could have never imagined. No longer was I an insecure, afraid, wounded little girl who desperately sought refuge in the arms of men. Now, in Christ, I had begun to fully bloom; each of my petals unfolding one at a time. I gleaned nourishment from the soil of God's enriching love. No longer was my identity wrapped up in others' approval of me. I began to accept that I am beloved of my Heavenly father, and this was my new identity. I accepted Christ's forgiveness and His promises; for this was my inheritance, and I no longer held myself hostage to past regrets. This is not to say that the next chapters of my life would come without challenges or difficulties; for there were many awaiting me on the road ahead. In the years to come, I would discover that struggles must be endured, battles produce endurance, and tears – well, tears are meant to water the garden of our souls. Though the place I now stood in was glorious, it was only the beginning of many more tests and trials to come. I had no inclination of the generational trauma that still lingered in my blood. God was preparing to blow my heart wide open, and the next dimension would require the refiner's fire.

The End

...or better yet, just the beginning.

Notes and Reflective Thoughts

Made in the USA
Monee, IL
09 October 2023

44282092R00085